ACRES *of* DIAMONDS

ACRES *of* DIAMONDS

DISCOVERING GOD'S BEST RIGHT WHERE YOU ARE

JENTEZEN FRANKLIN

Chosen

a division of Baker Publishing Group
Minneapolis, Minnesota

© 2020 by Jentezen Franklin

Published by Chosen Books
11400 Hampshire Avenue South
Bloomington, Minnesota 55438
www.chosenbooks.com

Chosen Books is a division of
Baker Publishing Group, Grand Rapids, Michigan

Printed in the United States of America

ISBN 978-0-8007-9867-3 (cloth)
ISBN 978-0-8007-9868-0 (paperback)

Library of Congress Cataloging-in-Publication Control Number: 2019949986

Cover design by LOOK Design Studio

Author represented by The FEDD Agency, Inc.

20 21 22 23 24 25 26   7 6 5 4 3 2 1

Dedicated to the people who saw a diamond in me . . .

My lovely wife, Cherise, for seeing who I could be and believing
in me enough to join me in this exciting adventure called life

My mom and dad, who encouraged me to pursue
my dreams in music and in ministry

Rachel Joyner for encouraging me to never give
up when I was just starting out in ministry

Bob Pauline, my piano teacher and mentor in music

Bishop T. F. Tenney, who was a diamond I lost that can
never be replaced until I see him again on streets of gold

Contents

Introduction

In 1869, near the banks of the Tigris River, Russell Conwell found himself on the back of a camel, listening to what seemed like the thousandth story told by his Arab guide. An attorney who had once attended Yale, Conwell was getting tired of his guide's vast treasury of stories, but, he later wrote, he was always glad he had listened to this one. His guide told of a man called Ali Hafed, who owned a large farm. I imagine he had a camel and a plow to work his land. He labored tirelessly for everything he had, day after day. In many ways, Ali Hafed was blessed, and he was content—until, that is, he had the pleasure of entertaining a stranger one day. An old priest came to visit, and by Ali Hafed's fireside, he told Ali Hafed about the discovery of diamonds in a distant land. With a handful of diamonds, the priest claimed, one could buy a whole country. With a mine of diamonds, one could place his children upon thrones.

That night, as Conwell explained when he shared this story, Ali Hafed went to bed a poor man. His contentment had evaporated, unseated by thoughts of the diamonds he did not have. The next day, he sought out the priest and begged, "Tell me where I can find diamonds."

The priest answered, "If you find a river between high mountains that runs through white sands, in those white sands, you will always find diamonds."

I want a mine of diamonds! became the cry of Ali Hafed's heart, and that day, he determined to chase his dream. He sold his farm. He hugged his wife and kids good-bye. And with a final, bold declaration, he said to them, "When I come back, we'll be fabulously wealthy. You'll be set for life."

Then Ali Hafed went off as a soldier of fortune, hunting for diamonds. He went to East Africa. No diamonds. He went to Palestine. No diamonds. He went to Europe. No diamonds. Finally, after consuming all of his wealth in search of greater fortune, Ali Hafed wandered into Spain. Still no diamonds. In Spain, this discontented man reached the point of such despair that he decided to end his life. He stood on a shore, watched a giant wave thunder toward him, and jumped into the raging waters, never to be seen again.

One day, the man who bought Ali Hafed's farm was leading his camel to a stream on his new property. It might, I imagine, have been the same camel Ali Hafed had owned. As the camel drank, a curious flash of light in the stream caught the man's eye. Looking closer, he reached down and pulled out a black stone. He noticed that when the sunlight hit it, the stone lit up with all the colors of the rainbow. The man thought to himself, *Pretty stone.* Then he walked back to his house, laid the stone on a mantel as a decoration and forgot all about it.

The next day, the same priest who had told Ali Hafed about diamonds stopped by. As he was talking to the new owner, the priest paused abruptly in midsentence. His eyes had fallen on the black rock sitting on the mantel.

Pointing to the stone, the priest exclaimed, "That's a diamond!"

The farmer shook his head. "Nothing of the sort. It's just a stone."

"I'm telling you," the priest insisted, "it's a diamond. Where did you get it?"

"I'll show you."

The priest followed the farmer to the garden by the stream. When they stirred up the white sand with their fingers, countless diamonds appeared, bigger and shinier than the first. The man who had bought the farm from Ali Hafed had inadvertently discovered the diamond mine of Golconda, the most magnificent diamond mine in history. In fact, crown jewels worn by royalty all over the world, including the Queen Mother in England, come from this very mine—from the same land, the same garden, the same stream and with the same camel that Ali Hafed had left behind.

Ali Hafed had traveled the world to find what he'd had all along. He never realized the potential of the place where he was. He never realized that he had been living on acres of diamonds. He thought, *If I could just go to Africa, or Palestine, or Europe, or Spain, I will find great worth.* All the while, diamonds lay right under his feet.

This story became part of a speech that Conwell was asked to give 6,152 times in his life, a fact included in *Ripley's Believe It or Not!* Years later, he turned it into a book, *Acres of Diamonds*, which became a bestseller. Conwell poured the profits into the newly built Temple University, founded in Philadelphia in 1884.[1] At the time I wrote this book, more than forty thousand students were enrolled at that fine institution—and it all began with this one story Conwell heard.[2]

What especially messed me up about this story is that the man who bought the same farm, the same garden, the same stream and the same camel that Ali Hafed thought were worthless turned them into acres of diamonds. You may feel the same way Ali Hafed did. You may think your life is worthless. You may think where you live is worthless. You may think your spouse is worthless. You may think your job is worthless. You may undervalue where you are and all you have. Know that there is hidden potential where you are right now. In your job. In the little town where you live. In your current marriage. In your family. In your church. The answer to your dreams may be right at your fingertips, if only you could see what is possible and believe.

Some people cannot fathom the unsearchable riches of Jesus that they are living in right now. They keep looking for something greater. They keep believing that there is something out there better than what they can experience in Christ. I am here today to tell you that if you know Jesus, your name is written in the Book of Life. If you have a Savior who has promised to never leave you nor forsake you, you are presently living in acres of diamonds.

I am going to give you a four-letter word that will change your life: *stay*.

Learn this word and live it. The grass is not greener somewhere else; you just have to learn to see, value and grow what you have, right where you are.

For you to get the most out of this book, you need to understand the type of staying I am talking about. There is a time for everything, as Ecclesiastes reminds us—a time to live and a time to die. A time to cry and a time to laugh. A time to scatter and a time to gather. A time to plant and a time to uproot. You get the point. There is no question that times change, and our lives along with them. We switch jobs. We move to a new city. We get married. We have another child. We attend a new school. We strive for a new dream. Life requires change. And certainly there are times when we have to shift in a new direction because the old one was unhealthy. Maybe we have to cut ties with toxic people or make a move to better the future of our children. That is all well and good. But there are other times when the place we are in feels fruitless and unexciting, and while we may be tempted to cut bait and run, we just do not feel the release from God. You might be in this very situation right now. Deep in your spirit, you know that you know that you know that you are not supposed to quit, give up or leave the place God has called you to.

You may feel stretched, or inadequate, or exhausted, or unqualified. You may feel as though nothing God has promised is coming to pass in that place, but you are not supposed to go somewhere else. I want to encourage you to push past the giving-up places. It's easy to quit, but it takes faith to go through.

When things get tough, don't sell out so cheaply. Don't believe the lies. Quit jumping from relationship to relationship. Quit running from church to church every time something happens you dislike. Quit hopping from job to job because you think it isn't giving you what you believe you are worth. If you leave, you may be giving up something that somebody else would give anything to have.

Know this: Inside of you are diamonds. In order for them to come out, it's going to take time. It's going to take setbacks. It's going to take disappointments. It's going to take trials. It's going to take going through challenges.

The same can be said of diamonds. It takes three things to make a diamond: time, extreme pressure and intense heat. Diamonds are made purely of carbon and are formed about a hundred miles beneath the surface of the earth. It takes high temperatures and extreme pressure for carbon atoms to bond to each other in a particular way that produces a diamond. Over time, this structure of carbon atoms locks into place and eventually grows large enough to produce a diamond.

Pressure, heat and time.

What does this mean to you today? Your trials serve a purpose, so don't run from them. Stay where you are and make it fruitful. When you stay in that place, you will learn more. You will grow more. You will become more. You will do more. God is turning up the pressure and the heat on you so that He can bring forth a diamond.

You cannot live for the Lord and not have trials. In fact, you cannot live on your own without having them. I tell people this all the time: Everything is better with Jesus, including trouble. If life is going to bring trouble with or without Jesus, you might as well choose Jesus. After all, He is the one who can carry you through. When you cannot make it, He can. He can conquer. He can triumph. God will not put more on you than you can bear. Dear reader, you are made of dirt. In other words, you're acreage. And only Jesus knows how to give birth to the diamonds of purpose and destiny in your life—no matter what you are facing right now. It will never happen without Him.

I think about the story in the Bible of the Prodigal Son. (Most of you probably know it. If not, you can read it in Luke 15.) I do not know what this young man was thinking when he left his father's house. I do know that he asked for his inheritance. I'm sure that he had some friends who were telling him something like, "Man, out there in the real world, everyone is having fun—parties like you've never experienced, freedom, unbelievable opportunities. You'll never find them if you stay here. You oughta leave your dad's house and get out there."

This young man bought into the lie that the grass was greener on the other side. But after leaving home, he lost everything. He ended up broke, eating slop with the swine in a pigpen. He finally woke up to the realization that everything he had ever wanted was already in his father's house. It wasn't out in the world. This young man was living on acres of diamonds he never should have left.

I have watched young people leave home because they're bored or feel restricted, thinking they can find fun and fulfillment elsewhere. I have watched people leave their marriages because they think they can find someone better with fewer problems. I have watched people leave their churches because they think they get nothing out of going or because someone has offended them. These people go off searching, trying this and that, because the enemy has convinced them that whatever they are looking for is out there. But it's not!

This is why the psalmist asked God to "open my eyes, that I may see wondrous things from Your law" (Psalm 119:18). The implication in this verse is that wonderful things might be all around you, but your eyes are closed. You cannot see them. I find that many people are living in spiritual poverty while they're surrounded by untold spiritual wealth. Maybe this describes you. Even as you read the introduction to this book, pray and ask God to open your eyes. You will find wonderful things in your life right now if you'll just quit looking at the half-empty part of the glass. God did not leave you without potential. He did not leave you without opportunity. You need to open your eyes to the good things.

That makes me think of Abraham and Lot, uncle and nephew. Lot knew Abraham had an incredible blessing on his life, and Lot was a smart guy. As his uncle became wealthy in livestock, silver and gold, Lot attached himself to Abraham. And Abraham increased in blessing—so much so, in fact, that his herdsmen and Lot's herdsmen started arguing. Conflict erupted. The tension got thick.

As Abraham was the elder, Lot should have submitted to Abraham. But Abraham was also a peacemaker. He did not want strife to infect his family. So he said to his nephew, "Let's separate. I'll let you choose all of the land in whichever direction you want to go."[3]

Lot looked over at the well-watered plains of the Jordan and saw the green grass and flourishing trees. He looked the other way and saw desert, tumbleweeds, cacti, rattlesnakes, rocks. He shook his head. "I don't want that," he said. Pointing to the well-watered plains of the Jordan, he continued, "I want that!" Suddenly, Lot looked a little further toward the horizon. The cities of Sodom and Gomorrah glowed like the lights of Las Vegas. "It looks like diamonds out there," he said. "I want that, too!" So Lot pitched his tent in the plains even as far as Sodom, and he began to chase after diamonds.

He never found them. In fact, the Bible tells us that over time Lot lost his wife. He defiled his relationship with his daughters. He lost his reputation. He lost his honor. He lost his place.

Abraham, on the other hand, settled in the desert, where it was hot and dry. *Pressure and heat.* I imagine Abraham looking at the ground and seeing sand. Many would call it worthless. A reminder that he was in a godforsaken place. But when Abraham looked at that sand, God gave him a vision for his life:

[Abraham,] I will make your descendants as the dust of the earth; so that if a man could number the dust of the earth, then your descendants also could be numbered. Arise, walk in the land through its length and its width, for I give it to you.[4]

Later, He told Abraham, "As are the stars of heaven, so will your seed be."[5] The sand represented Abraham's natural family that would come through Isaac. The stars represented his spiritual family, the Body of Christ. God gave Abraham a vision that he would give birth to a spiritual and a natural family. But it did not happen in the well-watered plains of Jordan. Nor did it happen in a city of lights. God opened Abraham's eyes in a hot and dry dust bowl.

What will you see when you ask God to open your eyes? When you begin to see what He sees in a place of heat and pressure, you can give birth to a vision that will change your life forever. Acres of diamonds.

Think about the thieves dying on either side of Jesus on the cross. One thief looks at Jesus and sees nothing but a man on a cross. He sees blood spurting from His side, His feet and His hands. He sees Him crowned with thorns. He hears the Master moaning, groaning and praying, "Father, forgive them." And this thief curses and mocks the Savior as he hangs there sentenced to die.

On the other side of the center cross, the second thief looks at the same thing the other guy saw. Same cross, same blood, same suffering, same wounds. But his eyes open to wondrous things. This man doesn't see a worthless piece of trash. He sees treasure. He sees acres of diamonds. And he begs Jesus, "Will You remember me when You enter Your Kingdom?" Jesus turns to him and says, "This day, you will be with Me in Paradise."[6]

Both men looked at the same cross, the same Jesus, the same trial, the same suffering and saw two different things. Isn't that something? See, it's about perspective. It's about vision.

Have you ever thought that you will finally be happy when you get such and such or when this or that happens? *When I get that house, then I'll be happy. When I get my breakthrough, then I'll be happy. When things settle down with my children, then I'll be happy. When I finally get that promotion, then I'll be happy.* You don't realize your greatest treasure is right here, right now—Jesus.

When Cherise and I came to the small town of Gainesville, Georgia, to pastor our first church, some people we knew wondered why we had settled on a no-name place in the middle of nowhere. "Why not go to a big city like Atlanta or Los Angeles?" they asked us. But when I got here, God opened my eyes to the potential of a church called Free Chapel. I saw, by faith, acres of diamonds. I saw a church that could touch the world. I saw precious people that loved God. I saw souls being saved. I did not see the small building on Browns Bridge Road; I saw a place where families were healed and marriages restored and lives changed. Funny, the 150-acre property we are on today used to be a dairy farm and a bee farm, a land literally flowing with milk and honey.

When you stop undervaluing where God has placed you, you will start to see the hidden potential of where you are.

But the owners didn't want it. They were tired of it. They saw one thing, but God saw another type of land flowing with milk and honey, and it fell into our hands. A place where thousands of souls would be saved and families healed.

There are acres of diamonds in the job you're tired of. There are acres of diamonds in the spouse you're annoyed with. There are acres of diamonds in the children who get on your nerves. There are acres of diamonds wherever you live, whether in a small town or a congested city. Quit waiting on somebody to give you a miracle, and recognize that you are sitting on acres of diamonds right where you are.

When you are stuck in a mentality of complaining, whining or making excuses, you are not in a position to discover diamonds. It is time to start praying, "God, open my eyes. Open my eyes to opportunities. Open my eyes to potential. Open my eyes to the relationships I have now. Open my eyes to the beauty of the place that You have me in now."

When you stop undervaluing where God has placed you, you will start to see the hidden potential of where you are—even in the trials. Even when it's hard. Even when the heat and the pressure are on.

God has placed you where you are, right now. Ask Him to open your eyes and see what is right in front of you. It is time to start digging in your own backyard.

1

Why Not Now?

In the United States in the late 1800s, keeping time was complicated. There was no single standard. You could tell the approximate time by looking at the position of the sun, which people had been doing for millennia before the invention of sundials and mechanical clocks. If the sun was directly above your head, it was noon and time to eat lunch. If the sun was setting over the horizon, it was bedtime. Most cities displayed a highly visible clock, like on a church steeple, but the time would be slightly different from city to city. Some were off from each other by a few minutes, others far more.

Railways operated independently on their own timetables. Similar to cities, each ran on a different time. This caused much confusion and led to dangerous conditions. Imagine the logistical nightmare in making travel plans or coordinating cargo deliveries—or, even worse, safety issues like two trains barreling toward each other from different directions because their schedules did not line up.

Finally, the heads of the major railroads collaborated to solve the problem. On November 18, 1883, they established the Standard Time system, which divided the United States and Canada into five time zones.[1] On that day, at exactly noon on the 90th meridian, workers at every railroad station reset their watches and clocks to reflect the new Standard Time within their designated time zone.

This was a win for the railways, but unfortunately for them, not everyone was happy with this new scheme. Many people were stubborn and chose to stick with whatever time they had established through whatever means. In some places, the gap between local time and Standard Time was as long as 45 minutes![2] Even some cities refused to switch to the new time. Arguments erupted. Towns were split. It took 35 years for Standard Time to be enacted by legislation for the entire United States and for people to fall in line with the new standard.

What about you? Have you fallen in line with God's clock? That's whose time we really need to know. We cannot make our own plans in life and expect everything to go according to our timetable. When it comes to following God, we need to stay in synch with God's timing. We need to have the same intentions as the psalmist who wrote "My times are in Your hand" (Psalm 31:15).

Get on God's Clock

The right timing is critical.

I've learned that God's timing rarely synchs with mine. As far as my personal preferences go, His timing usually doesn't coincide with mine. Our first entry into TV ministry was one such example. If it had been up to me, I would not have chosen that particular season. Our ministry had grown tremendously, which is always a good thing, but at the time, I felt stretched to the max. We had just moved into our new building and were continuing to furnish the space. We were working on eliminating debt we had accumulated. We were growing our staff. And in the midst of all the craziness, an opportunity popped up out of nowhere.

I had always felt called to television ministry, and even before I went to Free Chapel, I was making appearances as a guest speaker and musician on local TV stations throughout the country. I had my own ideas and my own plans for the perfect time to go on national television. And that particular moment definitely was not it.

One Saturday afternoon (I'm pretty sure it was in 1993), I received a phone call from R.W. Schambach, a famous evangelist with a huge following. He had been broadcasting daily on radio and TV for years. The day he called, R.W. was preaching in Atlanta. He told me that even though we had never met, he had heard about our church and that we had just moved into our new building. Then he asked if I would like for him to speak at our church the next day at our Sunday evening service. I was honored and thrilled and said of course I would!

The next night our sanctuary was packed out. There was a buzz in the air; fresh excitement and anticipation filled the auditorium. And R.W. showed up late. We didn't even have time to meet in person beforehand. I shook his hand for the first time on the platform in front of two thousand people. After I greeted everyone and said a few words, R.W. walked up beside me and whispered, "Can I obey God tonight?"

"Yes, sir," I replied.

Then he asked, "Can I take the service now?"

There was no question in my mind. "Absolutely!"

I sat down as R.W. began to preach, and powerfully. At the end of his message, he said, "I'm going to receive an offering tonight, but not for my ministry. The Lord impressed upon me that this young preacher, Jentezen Franklin, is supposed to be on TV to preach the Gospel. We're going to put him there. We are going to buy whatever he needs to get on TV."

Then, in one of the greatest miracles I have ever personally seen, one by one, people from the audience started bringing up to the platform $1,000 checks. In a matter of ten minutes, R.W. had raised more than $138,000. The money kept pouring in. The next week, we purchased cameras, lights, an editing suite and time on the local cable TV station every night from 7:30 to 8:30 p.m. Our TV ministry had just launched.

Here's the point: I had to get off my clock and get on God's clock. He knew the perfect timing for me. And I had to be obedient and do it—now.

When you feel God leading you somewhere or toward something, in these moments, you have to see the diamonds—not the stress, not the stretch, not the excuses, not the difficulties, not the impossibilities. Sometimes the greatest miracle God will do for us comes during the most inopportune time. It is because only in His power will we ever be able to pull it off.

As I look back over thirty years of ministry, it seems as though every major challenge we faced, like launching a new campus or starting a new outreach, stretched us past our limitations. More often than not, God presented us with opportunities when we felt the least confident in our flesh. Now, I am not talking about being foolish in pursuit of these things. I have, for example, always been financially conservative when making big decisions. But I believe God requires of us a faith that demands we trust Him more than what we think we can handle in our own ability. When He wants us to do something on His clock, He beckons, *Come out of your comfort zone and trust Me. You have enough to do it right now. I may not give you "the coast is clear" for the next two years, but right now, in this very moment, I want you to trust Me.*

In 2005 God spoke to me about starting an annual weekend conference for students around the world. As I began to envision it, I saw a few days in which young people would engage in incredible worship, learn from powerful speakers and grow deeper in God and His purpose for their lives. Our ministry had never done anything like that before.

When I talked to our team about it, they got excited. "Sounds amazing! Let's start working on it, and we can plan it for a year from now." It would take months, we knew, if not a year, to schedule popular bands and speakers for this kind of event. It would also require tons of time reaching out to churches and youth pastors and doing the marketing.

But God's timing was not a year from now. I felt an urgency to do it sooner. The idea consumed me; I just could not get it out of my head. I approached our team again and told them I wanted to schedule the conference for the beginning of summer, only a few months out.

Their eyes about bulged out of their heads. "But that's only months from now!" someone said.

"I know," I answered. "So let's make it happen however we need to make it happen."

As it turned out, on the weekend we had planned our conference, TobyMac, one of the most popular Christian artists at the time, needed to be in Atlanta for something. When we called his booking agency, our date fit perfectly with his schedule. Normally, getting him and his band on the calendar would have taken one year. God knew what He was doing. He knows the perfect timing.

Somehow, by the grace and goodness of God, we held our first-ever Forward Conference at our main campus with three thousand young people in attendance. It exceeded our wildest expectations. The next year, so many more students registered that we had to move the event to the Gwinnett Arena, now known as the Infinite Energy Arena, which seats more than 13,000 people. This conference has sold out in advance every year, and thousands upon thousands of teens have made decisions to follow Christ. Who knows if this would have happened had I stuck with man's clock instead of God's clock?

Had I not been obedient, for sure, we would have missed the perfect timing. I would have never realized the acres of diamonds that God would uncover not only for our ministry, but for the thousands of students who attended that first conference. Many times we want absolute certainty before we step out, a 100 percent money-back guarantee. But having this certainty takes the element of faith out of the equation, and you cannot experience success without risking failure. Sometimes faith is spelled R-I-S-K.

The Greek word for "opportunity" is *kairos*, which also suggests that something is time sensitive. Certain moments in life demand that you take action. Seize the moment or you will miss the opportunity.

It is usually not easy to see acres of diamonds, but if you ask God to open your eyes—and sometimes He'll open them without you even asking Him—you will know when an opportunity is being presented that requires you to move in that time. In 1 Chronicles 12, the sons of Issachar had their eyes open. They had an understanding of the times, and they knew what Israel ought to do and when. We need to have that same discernment, to know what we ought to do on God's clock.

Missed Opportunity

I'll admit I have not always seen the acres of diamonds in what looked like inopportune opportunities. Or rather, I may have seen diamonds, but I lacked courage to get on board with God's clock.

Many years back, after we had built our first building, I got a phone call out of the blue. I can't remember every detail of the conversation, but the person on the other end asked if I wanted to buy a local full-power television station for $3 million. Later, in person, he offered it for $2.5 million. It was a fantastic opportunity, and while $2.5 million was a lot of money, at the time it was a bargain. I felt God nudging me to say yes. Meanwhile everything in me was screaming no. We didn't have the money. We had maxed out our credit. Every penny we had was invested in the new facilities. When you're talking about building parking lots, buying furniture, outfitting offices, updating sound equipment and laying down flooring, it's pretty easy to spend $2 million, and quick. I knew the board and our staff were stressed to capacity with planning and budgeting for this new transition. How could I pile on one more thing?

Not only were we stretched financially, but spending $2.5 million for the station was just the beginning. A ton of overhead was involved. We would need to spend more money to hire the right staff and buy the right equipment to keep the station running. God may have been leading me in this direction, but I opted out. I just did not have the faith for it. I later learned it sold for $50 million.[3]

It is one of my biggest regrets. I would give anything to get that opportunity back. We didn't have $2.5 million lying around, but we could have stretched ourselves. It may have been a bit reckless, but it was possible. Not long after the offer was presented to me, the government enacted a must-carry regulation, which means that local-licensed television stations must be carried on a cable provider's system. The station I had said no to was not going to broadcast just in a local area; it would have reached the entire Atlanta metro region. I would have gotten all of Atlanta and more!

I'm not proud of my lack of trust. I should have had more courage. I should have listened to God. I should have tried harder. I should have somehow made it work. Instead, I chickened out. But I learned something: It is more important to stay on God's clock than trust my own.

A present opportunity plagued with problems is better than an awesome opportunity that has passed. If you wait too long, you can miss your destiny. You can miss your purpose. You can miss what God desired to give you. Now is the time. Today is the day.

> *A present opportunity plagued with problems is better than an awesome opportunity that has passed.*

I think of the woman who anointed the head of Jesus while He was at a dinner party. I picture her like a silent shadow, tiptoeing over the lounging disciples with her alabaster box. When she gets near Jesus, she breaks the box open, pours out expensive perfume all over His head and begins to worship Him. This perfume was costly, worth about a year's wages. In this holy moment, the other guests start to scold the woman. Knowing the hidden purpose behind this offering, Jesus rushes to her defense. "Let her alone," He commanded the judgey guests. "She has come beforehand to anoint My body for burial" (Mark 14:6, 8).

This woman got the timing right. She had an urgency inside of her that prompted her to think, *If I don't do this now, I'll never get another chance.* Shortly after, Jesus was arrested and would hang on a cross to die. Before He breathed His last, it is possible He could smell the aroma of the anointing the woman had poured over Him at just the right time.

Now is the time to break open your life and pour yourself over the Body of Christ.

The Power of Now

When we focus too much on what our own plans and timing should look like or the fear of what might or might not happen, we will miss the power of now.

Jesus knew this. In John 2 we read about the beginning of Jesus' earthly ministry. Jesus, His mom and His disciples have all been invited to a wedding. Suddenly, the wine runs out. When Jesus' mom discovers this social atrocity, she asks Him for help.

"What have I to do with this?" Jesus responds. "It's not my time yet."

But Mary is a discerning woman. She knows she has to push her son out into the ministry. Without a word in reply to Jesus, Mary turns to the servants, points to Jesus and says, "Do whatever He tells you."[4]

You know the story: Jesus gives His instructions and the servants fill six 20- or 30-gallon jugs with water. At the sight of its creator, the water blushes and becomes wine. Someone brings a sample out to the master of the feast, and the host is well pleased. "Every man at the beginning sets out the good wine," he praises the bridegroom, "and when the guests have well drunk, then the inferior. You have kept the good wine until now!" (John 2:10).

I want you to pay close attention to that statement: You have kept the good wine *until now.*

You probably know the popular saying "Save the best for last." If we're not careful, we can live our entire lives that way. Thinking that the blessing, the revival, the move of God, the miracle you need, the answer to your prayer is always out there, coming one day. Some day. Way out there.

But God does not just save the best for last. Sure, He can do that if He wants to; He's God. He can do anything. But He has also saved the best for *now*. We need to be careful that we're not living ten years out there, one day, someday. We can have victory now. We can have revival now. Lives can change now. Marriages can be restored now. Families can be reunited now. Addictions can be broken now. Breakthroughs can happen now.

The enemy wants to distract us from the power of believing, standing and trusting that right now is where the victory begins. The great days are not behind the Church. The great days are not behind you. God is not the God of the past. He is not sitting around waiting for someday to show His power and greatness.

God is the same yesterday, today and forever.[5] This means that if we comprehended the power of now, we would not have to wait. *You have kept the good wine until now.* God's best is not in the past, and it's not in the future. It's now.

Release Your Faith Right Now

Lazarus had been dead for a few days when Jesus finally showed up, and Martha had a few choice words for Him. "If You had only been here when my brother was alive, I know you could have healed him!"

Jesus looked at her with compassion and promised, "Your brother isn't dead for good. He will rise again."

Martha was looking ahead to one day. "I know that he will rise again in the resurrection at the last day," she replied.

"I am the resurrection and the life," Jesus said. "Whoever lives and believes in Me will never die. Do you believe this, Martha?"[6]

On one hand, Martha had mountains of faith—in the past. She knew if Jesus had been there when Lazarus got sick, Jesus could have healed him. She also had mountains of faith in one day. She believed that Lazarus would rise from the dead at the last day. On the other hand, what Martha did not have was faith in the present.

Jesus said, "*I am* the resurrection and the life." And He proceeded to resurrect Lazarus before Martha's eyes. Now is the time.

We need to decide when to quit saying, "One day, I'm going to live my purpose." "One day, I'm going to get our marriage fixed." "One day, I'm going to work through these problems." "One day, I'm going to take time for my family." "One day, I'm going to forgive." When are we going to realize that now is the time? This is the moment! Right here, right now.

Right now is all you have. This is where the power lies. And this is the key to releasing miracles in your life.

The word "now" spelled backwards is "won." We have to live knowing the battle is already won, even if we can't see it with our natural eyes. We have to praise God now, not when we see change in our circumstance. We need to trust God now, not when we understand everything. We must decide to believe God now, not when the manifestation comes. This is what faith is.

The Bible puts it like this: "*Now* faith is the substance of things hoped for, the evidence of things not seen" (Hebrews 11:1, emphasis added). The definition of faith is not someday. Faith *is*. It's now.

Start Living Today

Jesus Christ was the greatest gift the world has ever been given. The next greatest gift is now. Today. We are not promised tomorrow.

We are not promised another month. But you do have the incredible gift of right now. If you remember, Jesus was crucified between two thieves. I like to think one of them represented "yesterday" and the other "someday." Both want to steal your joy. If you're not careful in how you live and what you think, you will crucify "today" between those two thieves.

Yesterday is over, my friend. The past is past. It's done. You will never get it back. But if you allow it, that thief will steal the joy of today by getting you to live in the shame, the pain or even the success of yesterday. You will get stuck living back there instead of living right here, right now. Quit talking about one day or someday. You are right now living in acres of diamonds.

If the thief of yesterday fails in stealing your joy, the thief of someday will try and take it. And if you fixate on the future, what might happen or what might not happen, you are failing to realize the power of now.

"As your days, so shall your strength be."[7] In other words, God gives us enough grace to handle whatever day we are in. If you let your mind wander over into someday, worrying about the fear of the unknown, God doesn't have grace for you in that space. If you let your mind wander over into yesterday and allow yourself to get stuck because of what happened to you or what did not happen to you, God doesn't have grace for you there, either. God isn't *there*, He's *here*. Now. And He is not going anywhere. If you want to live in peace, if you want to stay out of depression, if you want to keep away from worry, anxiety and high blood pressure, then starting living today.

I love what the psalmist wrote: "This is the day the LORD has made; we will rejoice and be glad in it" (Psalm 118:24). I am not going to let the thief of yesterday or the thief of tomorrow steal my joy today. I am going to enjoy this day.

Your treasure is today. Yesterday is a cashed check, tomorrow a promissory note. Today is cash in the hand. Your miracle, your healing, your peace, your opportunity, your joy—all are one word away: *now*.

Learn to enjoy now. Learn to live in now. Learn to be obedient now. Learn to say yes to what God is calling you to do now. Focus on the now—that is where your influence is greatest.

Let's use the disciples as an object lesson. In Matthew 14, they find themselves in a boat when the waves are restless. They fight for control of the boat as it is tossed by waves and pressed upon by a mighty wind. Out of nowhere, Jesus shows up, walking on the water. But the disciples do not recognize Him. They think what they see is a ghost and cry out in fear. Why are they afraid? Because they aren't expecting Jesus, they are expecting an evil spirit. The disciples were waiting for the devil to show up. Is this you? Do you usually expect bad things? Or do you expect Jesus to show up in the middle of your storm or your need? The power in now is that you expect God to work in your life now, not someday.

Release your faith today.

The prophet Isaiah said, "Behold, I will do a new thing, now it shall spring forth; shall you not know it? I will even make a road in the wilderness and rivers in the desert" (Isaiah 43:19). Notice he says, "*Now* it shall spring forth." Sometimes you have to put your foot down and say, "Now." Release your faith today. Believe for God to move the mountains now.

When Jesus turned the water into wine, that miracle was the beginning of many more. You know when a miracle will begin for you? Not when you start seeing things change, but right now. When your faith says, "Now!" When you seek God with gratitude and praise and faith wherever you are, however you feel, in this very moment.

I want you to live in the power of now. It is time to enjoy. It is time to live. It is time to laugh. It is time to smile. It is time to give thanks. It is time to worship God. Are you putting off your miracle? Please, don't stay miserable and allow the enemy to crucify your today with yesterday or someday. Start all over again today. Ask God to make you a new creation.

There will never be a greater time to give your best, to give your all, to pour your life out on Him, than right now. Do today what you may not have a chance to do tomorrow. You cannot do anything about your past, but you can rewrite the rest of your life. It starts right here. Right now.

The author of Ecclesiastes wrote that a living dog is better than a dead lion.[8] This interesting statement means that as powerful as a lion is, if he's dead, it is nothing more than a lost opportunity. For him, it's over. I do not want to be a dead lion; I would rather be a living dog. As small of a dog as I may be, if I'm breathing, there is still life in me. I still have a chance. This is the day!

> *You cannot do anything about your past, but you can rewrite the rest of your life.*

Do you want to be set free from living in yesterday or living in someday? Do you want to start living in the power of now? Start rejoicing where you are. Set your heart and mind on Jesus, for He has saved the best for now. Attack whatever mountain is in your life with faith. Get on His clock. Lock your faith in and release it so you can live, laugh and enjoy life. We can't keep waiting for the perfect time—that time is now.

❖ 2 ❖

How Diamonds Are Born

Where you are standing right now may look more like a barren wasteland than acres of diamonds. You may be going through a tough season. Your 401(k) may have fallen like an egg from a tall chicken. You may have been laid off. Your child may have just been diagnosed with special needs. You may be walking through a health challenge or some other personally devastating landscape, and the weight of it all may be more than you can bear.

Be encouraged. God is digging in your field for the diamonds He has already birthed in you. Do you remember how diamonds are formed? Time, intense heat and extreme pressure. The diamonds that lie underneath the surface of your life are created in this same way. There is a reason for the heat. There is a reason for the pressure. So today, even right now, know that when we face problems, trials and adversity, God already has a plan in place to bring victory out of that situation.

This is why we don't run from the difficult times. We don't quit. We don't give up. You might not understand everything you are going through in this moment. You might not have answers to your questions. But unless you persevere through the hardship, you'll never receive the gifts, the blessings, the diamonds that God will bring forth through them. Trust me—I know what I'm talking about.

Blessings in the Battle

I was about sixteen years old, sitting toward the back in a Friday night camp meeting in a church in North Carolina. As a man named Ronnie Brock preached, I couldn't stop crying. I was being touched by the Spirit, but I did not realize it at the time. The Word of God declared in that meeting was tearing me out of my frame. "What is wrong with me?" I wondered as the tears fell.

That evening, God placed His hand on my life. I begged Him, "Use me. Give me revelation. Give me messages. Let me preach like Ronnie Brock. Let me reach people like that man."

I felt God speaking to my heart. *I hear you.*

Never in my wildest dreams did I expect what happened next.

Soon after that life-changing moment, huge blistering boils appeared all over my body, especially on my neck, back, chest and face. At times they would infect my nose, my eyes and my lips, causing them to swell to unsightly proportions. I was humiliated. Looking at my reflection in the mirror became a dreadful experience. Every day brought a new outbreak, it seemed, as doctor after doctor prescribed all kinds of creams and medicines. Nothing worked. The boils held fast to my skin like a nightmare I couldn't wake up from. This persisted for a whole year.

I remember going to school most days wearing a big puffy coat with a wide collar reaching up to my neck. I hoped it would hide the ugly boils, to no avail. The kids noticed. And they were cruel.

Some would poke fun at me, stirring up insecurity and sending my self-esteem into the gutter as I tried to ignore laughter when I passed by. Overnight, it seemed, I went from running with the popular crowd, loved by all, to a freak show. Nobody wanted to be seen with me.

This wrecked me. I fell into a deep pit of depression, and for a time I couldn't crawl out. Despair flooded me. I felt hopeless. I couldn't see a light at the end of the tunnel. It is a big deal at sixteen years old when all of your friends are having the time of their lives and you feel like a leper. I dreaded every public event I had to attend. I was alone, isolated and depressed.

I was also crying out to God in desperation, but the boils remained, and I felt accursed. It did not take long for suicidal thoughts to rise up and take hold in my mind from time to time. Giving up felt like the only option. With tears streaming down my face, I questioned God over and over. "What are You doing? Look at me! Look at what You did! I'm a freak!" I had asked Him to use me, and now I did not have the confidence even to stand up and look anybody in the eye. "You have devastated me!" I cried.

Into the life of this immature teenager wilting under confusion, anger and depression entered a woman of God named Rachel Joyner. She went to our church, and for some reason God had put me on her heart. She would fast and pray regularly for me. Other than my parents, Rachel was probably the biggest prophetic influence in my life—but I didn't realize it at first.

Rachel often gave me cards on which she wrote encouraging Scriptures. Most of them spoke directly to my heart and to my situation at just the right time, when I needed it the most. They usually came during my lowest points. Every time Rachel saw me, she would tell me things like, "Oh, Jentezen, one day you'll reach multitudes." "You have no idea how God is going to use you." "The anointing is about to increase on your life." I will never forget how her piercing eyes would fill with tears as she spoke with such conviction—and prophetic accuracy—exactly the kind of encouragement I was begging God for. Her words moved me to my core.

As time passed and it looked as though the boils were not going away any time soon, I began to open my heart to hear from God. I began to seek Him more. I didn't see His plan. I didn't see His purpose. But God knew that in the furnace of my affliction—in the heat and in the pressure—He was doing something in me.

Countless days, when the pus-filled boils oozed on my face, I would skip school out of embarrassment. I was quite good at covering my tracks. I would walk or have someone drive me to school, show up for homeroom and then skip out. My parents never knew. I always did my assignments and made decent grades. I had a key to my dad's church, and I'd stay there for hours, hiding under the sound booth in the balcony. No one saw me. Until school was over, I'd stay there, reading the Bible, listening to sermons through headphones on my cassette tape player and praying. People would walk through the church and never know a young boy was in the balcony under the sound booth with a Bible and a notebook, listening to sermons on tape. This was my testing ground, my field of diamonds. Intense heat and the trial of a lifetime. Diamonds of revelation were being born in my spirit. The call of God was being planted in my heart right there in His house, when I was all alone with Him. The Bible tells how Joshua lingered in the temple.[1] I can't help but think that is why Moses chose this young man to be his successor. In my wilderness experience, God was opening my eyes to who I was, who I was not, and whom He wanted me to become.

I did not realize the magnitude of what was happening at the time, but I was feeding my spirit. I was going to war for my future.

In the process, I was also growing closer to God in ways I believe would have never been possible had I not suffered from the boils.

During that year, other blessings unfolded. I began to develop my natural gifts. I had played the saxophone since I was twelve years old, but because I had isolated myself at home, I began to practice for hours each day. I believe this dedication led me to get a music scholarship for college. That summer I taught myself how to play the piano. Bob, an older friend and musician, showed me a few chords and mentored my musical talent. Toward the end of that year of sickness, I started teaching Sunday school for preteen boys at my church. I didn't know it yet, but it was the beginning of my ministry. God was answering my prayers in an unexpected way.

Finally, when the year drew to a close, a new medicine came out that cured the boils. My skin went back to normal, but my life was forever changed. It felt as though I was coming alive for the first time. Looking back, I know I would not even have entertained being in the ministry had it not been for that year of affliction. I am convinced I would have started partying with the wild crowd. I would have started doing things that would lead me far away from God. It was already starting to happen before the boils. I see today how much of that season has shaped the passion of my sermons through the years. Remembering the moments of hopelessness and how desperate I was for encouragement made me more sensitive to those going through rough times. It also made me more aware of young people who, in the eyes of society, don't have the right look or right clothes, whom others ridicule or deem unworthy. This experience drew my heart to the overlooked, because I was that person.

When you face a trial, know you are not going to stay in it forever. The pain will not last forever. The heartbreak will not last forever. The anxiety will not last forever. The fear of the unknown will not last forever. The despair will not last forever. God brings an end to darkness.

God can open your eyes to acres of diamonds in the midst of your affliction, in the midst of the heat and the pressure. Only He can take a mess and turn it into a message. Only He can take a test and turn it into a testimony. Only He can take adversity and turn it into advancement.

The devil comes to kill, steal and destroy. And sometimes God allows pain, suffering and loss to come our way. But what the enemy inflicts and what God may allow will be used in some way, somehow, for God's glory. All things work together for the good of those who love God (see Romans 8:28). That is *all* things. Not some things. Not just good things. *All* things. Hell is not in charge of anything. Even if the enemy sent it, God will transform the thorn in your flesh. God will use it. And, as Paul said in 2 Corinthians 12:9, God's grace is sufficient.

Diamonds in the Dirt

You could say that my affliction of boils was a strangely wrapped gift. Many blessings come that way, actually. It is not easy to realize this, however, when you're in a tough season.

An old story of such a blessing goes something like this:[2] A young man from an affluent and notable family was a few months away from graduating high school. He made clear to his dad that he wanted a sports car as a graduation gift, something fast and flashy. All the other parents in the neighborhood had purchased vehicles for their children upon graduation, so he assumed his mom and dad would follow suit. Besides, he knew they had the money for it.

He and his dad spent months looking at cars, hopping from dealership to dealership until the son found the perfect one. When graduation day came, the father asked his son to come into his study. When the young man walked in, he noticed a beautifully wrapped package tied with a red bow on the desk. The father smiled, pushed the gift across the desk toward his son and said, "This is my graduation present to you."

The son was confused. This was not what he had expected. Where was the sports car? He unwrapped the gift and took the lid off the box. Inside was a Bible. Infuriated, the young man put the lid back on the box and shoved the gift back across the desk.

"Thanks, Dad," he said, his voice heavy with sarcasm. "Thanks a lot!" The young man stormed out of his dad's study, went to his room, packed up his things, and walked out of the house. He never came back. And he never saw his father again.

Years later, news of his father's death brought him back home. He sat down at the same desk in the same study in which he had refused his father's gift. As he rummaged through some paperwork, his eyes fell on his father's gift. He opened up the box, pulled out the Bible and started flipping through its pages. Out fell a check, in the exact amount of the car he had chosen for his graduation gift.

The son rejected his father's gift because it was packaged in a way he did not expect. Wouldn't you hate to miss out on an incredible gift because it came wrapped in an unexpected package? We expect diamonds to show up in a black velvet box, but they never come from God that way.

We serve a God who often sends His children strangely wrapped gifts. They certainly do not appear to be gifts. They look like trials. A failed relationship. Conflict at work. Conflict at home. A job loss. Health trouble. Mental affliction like anxiety and depression. And

41

if you do not wait on the Lord, trust in Him and stand in faith, you will, full of disappointment and bitterness, push the gift back the heavenly Father's way:

"This is not what I was praying for, God."

"This is not what I was expecting or believing for."

"This is not what I wanted."

"Take it back. I don't want it."

When we reject God's gift, we reject His plan and purpose for our lives. We abandon the very acres of diamonds that He has called us to.

The Bible is full of people who received strangely wrapped gifts. Take Job. God was ready to do something incredible in his life. He was about to bring Job wealth, a wonderful family, a ton of property and much success. In fact, God promised to bless him with double. But think about the strangely wrapped gifts that showed up on Job's doorstep first.

Package number one comes along: All of Job's flocks are stolen or burned and all his servants killed. Package number two, perhaps the most hideous a parent could get: All of his children die. Job's got nothing. No household. No kids. No Bible. No church. No Jesus. All he can say is, "The Lord gave, and the Lord has taken away; blessed be the name of the Lord" (Job 1:21). At least Job had his health, his friends and his wife, right? Well, it doesn't take long for Job to get sick. Then his wife tells him to "curse God and die." Finally, his friends accuse him of being a hypocrite, suggesting God is punishing him because he did something wrong.

Still, Job had God, right? It didn't feel that way to him. "Look, I go forward, but He is not there, and backward, but I cannot perceive Him; when He works on the left hand, I cannot behold Him; when He turns to the right hand, I cannot see Him."[3]

Have you ever had a season like that? I've had many.

Surrounded by these packages of suffering and pain, Job said something I love: "I know that my Redeemer lives."[4] What Job was really saying was, "Not even heaven can shake my confidence."

Now, hell cannot shake our confidence because it's obvious when the devil is doing something. But what about when God allows terrible things to happen? What about the questions we ask then? *Why didn't God save my spouse? Why did God permit my child to suffer? Why did the cancer come back? Why did my husband abandon me? Why? Why? Why?* Job asked similar questions. But ultimately, he put his trust in God. "I know my Redeemer lives," he determined, "and one day when I've come forth from this wreckage, I will be refined as pure gold, and I'll see Him for myself." That is a diamond right there!

Job made it through the trial. And God promised to give him double of everything he lost. Double livestock. Double business. I find it interesting that God doubled everything Job had except his children. God gave him ten more children, the same number as he had had before. Why? Because he did not lose them; they were alive and well in heaven.

I want to encourage you to receive God's strangely wrapped gifts. Accept them. Even if they hurt. Even if they feel lousy. Even if you don't understand them.

God Will Use Your Trials

God had a high and mighty dream for Joseph as well, and it came in strangely wrapped packages.

The first one shows up in Joseph's life when his brothers rip off his coat of many colors and kidnap him. Then they throw him into a pit and later sell him into slavery. Joseph ends up in Egypt, working in the house of Potiphar. There, Potiphar's wife falsely accuses him of raping her. He is thrown into prison for years for a crime he did not commit. Another strangely wrapped gift.

While in prison, Joseph makes friends with a butler and a baker from the palace. They each have strange dreams. Joseph, having a special gift, offers to interpret them with one caveat: "Remember me when you get out of prison." They promise they will, and Joseph interprets their dreams. The butler and the baker get brought before Pharaoh, and Joseph's interpretations prove correct. Yet neither one of them keeps his promise.

There comes a day when Pharaoh has a dream that no one could interpret. The butler finally pipes up. "There's a man in the dungeon who can interpret dreams. He interpreted mine, and it came true." And within 24 hours, not only is Joseph released from prison but Pharaoh is so impressed with him that he makes Joseph second in command over all of Egypt. This seems sudden, but the blessing is wrapped in a package that is strange and unusual.

Twenty-some years after Joseph's brothers had left him for dead, they stand before him in the Egyptian palace. Now the roles are reversed—his brothers are the weak ones and Joseph the strong. The men tremble before him, fearing he will settle the score and throw them into a pit of his own making. But he doesn't. And in his explanation, we find his inspiration.

As his brothers weep on their faces before him, Joseph says, "Do not be afraid, for am I in the place of God? But as for you, you meant evil against me; but God meant it for good, in order to bring it about as it is this day, to save many people alive."[5]

Joseph is so touched by compassion and the healing of the many wounds in his own life that he can look at his own brothers, who had done him terrible wrong, and say, "You meant what you put me through for my evil, but God meant it for my good." Wow!

Asking God for something is not just about Him giving you what you ask. It's about Him preparing you to be able to handle it. It's in the suffering, the hurting and the waiting that God can begin to mold and shape your soul, your heart and your ego. This does not happen in the high times. This does not happen when everything is going great and God is answering every prayer the way that you want. It's about you becoming what He has called you to become. It's about God being able to trust you with what you are asking Him to give you.

It's also about Him using what we go through to minister to others and bring glory to His name. I do not think my ministry would be the same today had I not been afflicted with the boils nor experienced other trials in my life through the years. Each of us endures seasons of suffering, but God uses these times to bring comfort, peace and faith to others through us.

> *Asking God for something is not just about Him giving you what you ask. It's about Him preparing you to be able to handle it.*

Paul understood this revelation: "I want you to know, brethren," he wrote, "that the things which happened to me have actually turned out for the furtherance of the gospel" (Philippians 1:12). He was saying, "I know the stuff that comes into my life, whether God sent it or He allowed it, is going to be transformed into good. A diamond is going to fall out of these strangely wrapped gifts to free people in Christ, or heal them, or open the door of blessing for them. So I'll take pleasure in my gift wrappings, in my suffering, in my tribulation. I'll come out stronger. The strength of Christ will be made perfect in my weakness, because everything that's happened to

45

me has happened to further the Gospel in my family, my life, my world."

The point of your existence is not just about you having a nice, sweet, idyllic life. Sooner or later, storms will hit you and your family. Don't be the kind of Christian who lacks depth and substance and does not know what to do when trouble comes. Don't throw a temper tantrum. Don't shove the gift back to the Father. Remind yourself that He will work everything for good. Remind yourself that God digs in the dirt to bring forth a diamond. Remind yourself that through these things, your faith will grow.

Years ago I preached a sermon from the book of Daniel about Shadrach, Meshach and Abednego. I called it "Three Plus Fire Equals Four." These three Hebrew men were thrown into a fiery furnace by Nebuchadnezzar, the king of Babylon, because they refused to bow down to his image. But the men were not burned alive. When King Nebuchadnezzar peeked into the flame-filled room, he was shocked to find a fourth man, who looked like the Son of God, walking around with them. My point? Sometimes the only way to get to Jesus—that fourth man—is to go through the fire.

I did not know it at the time, but a certain man and his wife were sitting in church that morning. Some months before, the man had been in a terrible fire and had suffered third-degree burns over half of his body. Multiple surgeries and skin grafts followed. That particular Sunday, the man looked at his wife and said, "We've got to go to church."

This was a surprise to his wife, for they had not been to church for a long time. She looked at him, dumbfounded, and asked where he wanted to go. And as the Lord would have it, he named the church where I was speaking that morning.

After listening to my message about walking through the fire to get to Jesus, this man rededicated his life to the Lord. His salvation and that of his family came in a strangely wrapped package.

When I talked with this man after church that day, he showed me his arms. They were wrapped in fresh bandages that covered severe burns. With tears in his eyes and gratitude in his heart for the experience of God's amazing grace, he told me he found the gift of Jesus through these strange wrappings and wounds from the fire. Wow!

We may not understand some of the things that happen to us in this life on earth, but God promises that all things work together for them that love Him and are called according to His purpose.[6] *All* things. There is nothing that has been done to you that God cannot make work out for you if you put it in His hands.

How to Outlast Your Toughest Season

David has some great revelation and promises about what to do through the tough times of life. Psalm 1:1–3 offers some of this insight:

> Blessed is the man who walks not in the counsel of the ungodly, nor stands in the path of sinners, nor sits in the seat of the scornful; but his delight is in the law of the LORD, and in His law he meditates day and night. He shall be like a tree planted by the rivers of water, that brings forth its fruit in its season, whose leaf also shall not wither; and whatever he does shall prosper.

The thing I love about David is that he is not always happy. When you study this man in Scripture, you find times when he's riding high and other times when he's low and wiped out. It is important to understand that David is not a one-dimensional person. Through the course of his life, he experienced a full range of emotions, just as we do. Now think about David's life for a minute. This young man was anointed to be the king of Israel. But before he was put on the throne, he was rejected by his brothers. He was attacked by a lion and almost killed by a bear. He was so hated by King Saul that Saul hunted him down like a dog and tried to murder him multiple times. All this was preparing David for what he was anointed to do. Know this: God has already prepared you to outlast your toughest season.

Sow the Word into Yourself

When you are going through a tough season, you will hear a voice in your head constantly telling you to give up. Trying to convince you that you won't make it, pushing you to quit. Even to this day, I hear that voice in my head.

David gives us a powerful key in the Scripture above. He tells us to meditate on God's Word day and night. In the Hebrew, the word *meditate* means to "utter or speak"—in other words, self-talk. You are supposed to self-talk the Word of God through your tough seasons.

When the enemy attacks and tries to defeat, depress or humiliate you, that is when you begin to fight back with your words:

"The Word of God says I am blessed and highly favored of God" (see Ephesians 1:3).

"I am a child of God and He loves me" (1 John 3:1).

"I have never seen the righteous forsaken or begging for bread" (Psalm 37:25).

"God brings an end to my darkness."

"I won't always be down."

"I won't always be lonely."

"I won't always be needy."

"I am somebody."

"I am going somewhere."

"I'm going to do something big with my life for Jesus Christ."

You've got to start telling yourself what the Word says about you. Inside of your head is either blessing talk or cursing talk. Overcoming talk or undergoing talk. Victory talk or defeat talk. You've got to talk God's Word to yourself through tough seasons.

When Rachel came into my life at the point of my deepest depression, this is what she inspired me to do. When I began to realize the power of Scripture, I began to change my future talk. I told myself who I was according to what God says, not what I thought about myself or what others said about me. Your self-talk sets you up for joy or misery. You can tell where your faith is by what comes out of your mouth.

The first way to outlast your toughest season as a blessed man or woman is to meditate on the Word of God and not let it depart from your mouth.[7] This is why self-talk matters. Confess what God says over your life!

Be Planted Like a Tree

The second way to outlast your toughest season is to be planted like a tree. What kind of tree? A tree that goes through more than one season. A tree that in one season is fruitful and produces for months and in other times outwardly looks barren. The leaves are gone. The branches are empty. But it remains planted. It survives during this season so it can be fruitful for the next.

Think about the purpose of your freezer. You put things in there that you want, just not right now. You want to enjoy the food you are freezing at the right time. When you go through a season that looks ugly, barren and fruitless, if you will stand and outlast the cold, a time will come when God will thaw you out. And in that very area that looked hopeless, you will be fruitful. In that very area of barrenness, you will produce. In that very area of despair, you will make hell pay.

But you've got to remain planted—in the Word. In the Church. In prayer. In marriage. In family. You may go through different seasons, but as a tree your job is to stay planted.

After the devil fell from heaven, God cursed him. The enemy has no place of planting. There is no place he really belongs. Job 1:7 tells us he moves to and fro on the earth, walking back and forth on it. We also know from 1 Peter 5:8 that he prowls around like a lion. He is not rooted anywhere!

Satan knows your potential, and his greatest fear is that you will discover who you really are, what you're really worth, and where you're really headed.

When you do not plant yourself in a church, in fellowship with other believers and, most importantly, in God, you are doing the same thing. You are moving "to and fro." That is a curse!

The blessing of the Lord is found when you are planted in relationship, in the covenant of marriage or in the house of God. Do not forsake the power of partnership. If you are in a tough season, stay planted. Don't move. Stay in your marriage. Stay in your church. Stay in prayer. Stay in the Word. Dig in your own fields. Stay where God has planted you.

We won't understand everything we go through in this life. Some of the trials we go through are hard. Some of them really hurt. Some of them break our hearts. But "in everything give thanks; for this is the will of God in Christ Jesus for you" (1 Thessalonians 5:18). Notice it doesn't say to thank God _for_ all things but _in_ all things. Whatever situation you are in right now, give thanks. Turn your pain and your tears into praise. Turn your suffering into a statement of faith that says, "God, I trust you even when I don't understand you. I trust you when I don't have any explanation for what I'm going through. I know my Redeemer lives!"

When your situation is not what you expected or what you wanted, whatever the pain, whatever the tears, whatever the heartache, stand firm in your faith, and trust in God's love. Maybe you are thinking, _I'll be glad when these attacks are over and I can settle down._ Dream on! If you do anything significant for God, you'll attract attacks like a magnet. You are too valuable to the Kingdom. Satan knows your potential, and his greatest fear is that you will discover who you really are, what you're really worth, and where you're really headed.

3

The "Stay Here" Command

A round 1840, Edmund McIlhenny moved from Maryland to Louisiana to seek fortune. He found much success in the banking industry. A foodie and an avid gardener, McIlhenny was beside himself when someone gave him seeds of *Capsicum frutescens* peppers that had come from somewhere in Mexico or Central America.[1] One account suggests that a soldier from the Mexican-American War gave him some dried peppers from Mexico. However he got them, McIlhenny fell in love with the spicy flavor and saved the seeds. What we know for sure is that this successful banker sowed the pepper seeds in his sugar plantation on Avery Island. A major tourist attraction today, it wasn't really an island but a gigantic salt dome.

When the Civil War came to Louisiana, McIlhenny, along with other families on that island, fled to other places, mostly Texas. When the war was over, he came back home. As McIlhenny looked around what had been a beautiful sugar plantation, all he saw was devastation. The plantation destroyed. Their house plundered. Fields wiped out. Crops wrecked. Fences burned down.

Equipment smashed. And then, in the midst of this devastation, his eyes fell on life. Pungent, fruitful, growing life. The only thing that survived in this barren wasteland were the hot pepper plants. They were everywhere!

Seeing the wreckage of the island, other families made plans to leave. They probably said something like, "Everything here is ruined! There's nothing left. We can't survive in this place." So they took off, likely to New Orleans or back to Texas.

McIlhenny, however, stayed.

With his home in ruins, his wallet empty from a collapsed economy, without a job or a prospect of a job, this man had an idea. "I have plenty of salt. I have peppers in abundance. And I've got some vinegar in an old whiskey barrel somewhere." And in 1868, McIlhenny mashed up the peppers with the salt, let the concoction sit for a while, then added the vinegar.[2] In that moment, he had created a hot sauce that no one in that region of the country had ever tasted. The sauce was so good, he and his wife started putting it on everything. Considering how bland the diet in that area was at the time, McIlhenny's little sauce took food to the next level. He was on to something.

One day, he found tiny perfume bottles someone had thrown in the dump. He took these bottles, cleaned them out and put sauce in each one. He started giving them away to his friends and family. They loved it and asked for more. Then he gave them as samples to wholesalers. They loved it and asked for more. He started selling the sauce in restaurants in New Orleans. Soon orders poured in. Everyone was asking for McIlhenny's sauce, or, as we know it today, Tabasco Original Red Pepper Sauce.

This privately owned hot sauce company boasts 20 to 25 percent of the market today and has an estimated net worth of more than two billion dollars. Each day, more than 750,000 bottles are made, labeled in 20-plus languages and dialects and distributed to restaurants and retailers in more than 160 countries. It's also a family company, a five-generation organization. All this from a man who had nothing but hot peppers—and who stayed.

Imagine if McIlhenny had looked at his devastated property and took off like everyone else. Five generations would have missed this megablessing—five generations! I wonder what we miss when, instead of staying planted, we hightail it toward the easy road.

Stay Where You Are

Let's look at this through a spiritual lens. How well do you respond to the Lord's "stay here" command?

Let me put it another way. When you are praying for something and nothing is happening, what do you do? When no breakthrough comes, do you move on? When you are sowing in a place or in someone or in something God has called you to, but it's producing nothing, what then? However you answer these questions, I want to give you the answer you ought to have.

If God has called you to a certain place, to a certain relationship, to a certain job, to a certain dream, to a certain community, no matter how unfruitful it may look to you on the outside, you stay right where you are. You don't quit. You don't pack your bags. You don't go somewhere else that looks better. You stay. When everyone else has left, you stay. When you are in a drought and there is no sign of rain, you stay.

In Genesis 26 we read about Isaac, Abraham's son, who is living in a place called Gerar during a time of famine. God warns him not to go to Egypt but to *stay where he is*. He promises Isaac that He will bless him beyond measure. He will perform the vow He had given his father, that his descendants would multiply as the stars of heaven. So Isaac stays. He also sows into the land. In that same year, Isaac reaps a hundredfold.

We in the blessed country of America do not really comprehend what a famine is. We complain about "starving to death" if we miss lunch. I remember visiting Haiti after it was struck by an earthquake in 2010. I saw hundreds of people, adults and children, who had not eaten for weeks. I remember holding a tiny baby in my arms. Her belly was horribly swollen, and her hair was brittle and turning orange, symptoms of severe malnutrition. It was unbelievable. The tears. The sadness. The hunger. The flies. The devastation. The disease. The lack of water. The unsanitary conditions. This is what happens when famine strikes. No one has food. No one has water. No one has anything. And it was in this kind of situation in Isaac's time that God told him to stay right where he was.

I find it interesting that years before, Abraham went through a famine as well.[3] He chose to leave the Promised Land and flee to Egypt. Abraham may have made a mistake, but Isaac doesn't repeat it. He doesn't do what his daddy did. Gerar may not have been a perfect place or nearly as beautiful as Egypt, but it was where God wanted Isaac.

It would have been much easier for Isaac to leave Gerar and go over to Egypt himself, where the food was plentiful and everyone was having a great time. Seems that whenever we go through stuff, we can always find someone living somewhere else who is doing very well. And sometimes they aren't even living for God! Ever feel that way as a believer? As though you are living in famine in the Promised Land and everyone else is prospering in Egypt? I have, and I'll tell you what I do about it: I stay where I am.

This is in sharp contrast to what happened when a woman named Naomi found herself in a famine in Bethlehem. In Hebrew,

Bethlehem means "house of bread." There is something wrong when the house of bread is breadless. So Naomi, her husband, Elimelech, and their two sons escaped the famine by leaving Bethlehem, the house of bread. They traveled to Moab, a country that was approximately 25 miles away—not very far at all. Leaving seems a very logical thing to do when you are in a famine and everyone is starving, and all the other families are running off somewhere where food can be found.

When you're in Bethlehem, though—when you're in God's house, the house of bread—even when it is breadless, you don't leave. You stick it out and stay. I don't care how called you are to a place, a business, a marriage, a job, or a calling; hard times are going to come. Lean times. You will go through battles. This is just as true in your relationship with God. Sometimes even when you are where God has destined you, it feels spiritually dry. You cannot hear Him. You cannot feel Him. You may go to church. You may read the Bible. You may do all the right things. You just don't feel the goose bumps of His presence. Yet, through all these things, you must persevere.

If you know you are called to a certain house of bread, when it's breadless, you stay there until the bread comes back. Because it's only a matter of time before it does.

We are too quick to jump ship and hop to somewhere else that looks much better. We are always looking for something out there that is easier, or prettier, or younger, or less complicated, or has a better view or zip code. But here's the thing: If you know you are called to a certain house of bread, when it's breadless, you stay there until the bread comes back.

Because it's only a matter of time before it does. Sometimes God will let you go through famine to prove you, to test you, to see what is in your heart. When this happens, stay put until the bread comes back.

When Naomi and her family got to Moab—which, by the way, was known as a cursed place—tragedy struck. Elimelech died. Then one son died. Next, the other. Naomi found herself in Moab with only her two daughters-in-law. Eventually, Naomi heard there was bread in Bethlehem, so she and her daughter-in-law Ruth returned to the city she had left. Imagine that. Naomi and her family traded three funerals for one famine. Sometimes it is better to go through your worst day where God wants you than your best day anywhere else.

This Is the Place

It is easy to think that God is going to do something great in distant places, but He can do a mighty work in a dust bowl. When it looks like your dream or your resources are drying up, God will be with you. And He will help you.

Isaac knew this. He didn't let a dust bowl of a land intimidate him or keep him from being obedient to God's command. I love what he does—in the midst of the famine, as he is prospering, he begins to dig wells. Abraham had done the same years back, but the Philistines had stopped them up. Isaac seeks out those same wells and begins to dig. When he finds the first well of running water, the Philistines start contending with him. But that conflict does not keep Isaac from digging more wells. He calls that first well Esek, or "contention," and starts digging the next. The Philistines show up and begin to quarrel with him again. Isaac doesn't care. He doesn't say, "This is too hard! I need to go somewhere else." He stays and calls that second well Sitnah, or "hatred." When he digs the third well, the Philistines finally realize Isaac isn't going anywhere. He calls that place Rehoboth, or "roomy space," because "the LORD has made room for us, and we shall be fruitful in the land" (Genesis 26:22). I love this guy's persistence. Isaac determined to keep digging wells until he got himself a roomy place!

You need to send that same signal to the enemy. Stand firm where you are. Keep digging where you are. If God has called you to a certain place that looks like a dust bowl, stay put and say, "I'm not leaving. This is the place." If others are unkind, stay faithful. If you feel all alone, keep trusting. If it does not seem that the promise is coming, keep believing.

When Moses and the people of Israel were in the wilderness, in one of many instances, the people started to whine and complain.[4] "We're dying of thirst!" "We're starving!" "There's nothing to eat or drink!" "We're tired!" "It's hot!" Plenty were thinking, *This is ridiculous. Why on earth did we listen to Moses and leave Egypt? Let's go back.*

But God said, "This is the place." And in the middle of the wilderness, without food and without drink, God told Moses to stay. More than that, He told him to do something else: "Get out the Levitical choir, Moses. It's time to start singing!"

Here's how I imagine this pathetic scene. These people are out in the desert. Dust everywhere. Hot as fire. They have been on the move for a while and are weary. But the choir gets up and starts singing:

> Spring up, O well!—Sing to it!—
> the well that the princes made,
> that the nobles of the people dug,
> with the scepter and with their staffs.[5]

And as they sing, I can picture the priests as they start tapping the dry dirt with their staffs. *Tap. Tap. Tap.* All they are doing, it seems, is creating a cloud of dust. Some start coughing. Others start choking. But they continue to pound the earth, and the choir continues to sing. I can imagine one of the priests pounding his staff into the ground, but this time it gets stuck. He can't pull it out of the ground. So he calls Moses over. Both of them grasp the staff with all their might and jerk that rod out of the ground. But wait—the end of the stick is dripping wet. Moses says, "Hit it again!" And with the background of "Spring up, O well," water starts gushing out of the dry ground.

This is the place!

If God has called you somewhere, even if your situation is plagued with problems, this is the place.

God works in unusual places. Surprising places. Barren places. Jesus Christ came as a root out of dry ground. Lazarus was resurrected four days after he died, smelling of rot and decay. God found Moses in the desert. He found Job in the trial. He found the three Hebrew children in the fiery furnace. He found Daniel in the lions' den. He found Elijah under a juniper tree, wanting God to kill him. God found Jeremiah in a pit, Peter in a prison and Paul in a storm. God uses unusual places to bring His glory out of them.

Do the best you can with what you've got.

If you are in an unusual place, don't run. Don't pack your bags. Stand and sow into that land. Do the best you can with what you've got. God is faithful; He will not leave you breadless in the place He has called you to.

This is the place.

What Is Tattered Can Be Restored

It might be that you were once on top of the world, holding a dream in your hand with high hopes and great expectations. Today your dream has been tattered. Maybe you failed. Maybe something happened that was not your fault. There is still treasure to be found in that place. God can still bring forth a diamond. Don't give up! God is a restorer of the place of broken dreams.

Billionaire real estate mogul and art collector Steve Wynn is known for resurrecting and expanding the luxury casino and hotel industry in Las Vegas in the 1990s. He lined the streets of that city with remarkable resorts like the Mirage, the Bellagio and the Wynn. Known also for his love of art, some of his collection, pieces of which are worth millions of dollars, are on display in his hotels.

In 2001, Wynn acquired a famed painting by Picasso. He purchased *Le Rêve*, French for "The Dream," for an undisclosed amount, estimated to be about $60 million. It is said that Picasso, fifty years old at the time, painted it in one afternoon in 1932. The woman in the beloved work of art is his twenty-something girlfriend. Wynn loved this painting so much that he considered naming one of his hotels after it. Five years later, he decided to sell *Le Rêve* to a friend of his, Steven Cohen. Cohen had coveted this painting for a long time. The two businessmen agreed to a sale price of $139 million. At the time, this was the most expensive piece of art ever purchased. A few weeks later, Cohen hired a professional art inspector to evaluate the condition of *Le Rêve*. Finding it to be in excellent shape and worth every penny, she approved the sale.

The next weekend, the real estate mogul threw a dinner party at his hotel, the Wynn, for some friends who were in town from

New York City. His guests included celebrities like Nora Ephron, Barbara Walters and the former editor of *Vogue*.

As the famous crew wined and dined, Wynn told his guests about the upcoming sale of his beloved painting. Intrigued by this work of art, they asked to see it. Wynn invited his guests to his office the next day, where he had recently moved *Le Rêve* from the hotel lobby.

The next day, Wynn's friends gathered in his office to marvel at the painting. It was on display on a wall surrounded by other famous works of art, including a Matisse and a Renoir. As his guests oohed and aahed over Picasso's depiction of his dream, Wynn began to give them a mini art lesson about the famous painter and this particular work of art. He stood with his back to *Le Rêve*, celebrating this dream on one of the last nights he would have the painting in his possession.

Suffering from an eye disease that affects his peripheral vision (and not even thinking about what he was doing), Wynn took a few steps back and made a gesture with his right hand, unintentionally whacking the masterpiece. A distinct ripping sound echoed through the room. Wynn had punctured the painting with his right elbow.

Everyone in the room gasped as they stared at the two-inch tear in the canvas.[6] The $139 million dream was shredded. Torn. Ruined.

Later that week, Wynn's wife took the ripped painting to New York to meet with his art dealer. They both agreed the deal was off until the full extent of the damage could be determined. The sale contract was ultimately terminated, and the insurer of the painting dropped the value of the painting to $85 million, a $54 million loss.[7]

But the story wasn't over. Wynn found a renowned art restorer who agreed to fix the painting to its original condition. I like to imagine this art surgeon said something like, "Mr. Wynn, I believe that I can repair this torn dream. As a matter of fact, I'm sure I can, and when I get through with it, I'm going to restore it so that it's going to look better than it did before it was ever torn."

Wynn decided to keep the painting after this art restorer fixed it. Six years later, however, he sold it to Cohen for $155 million.[8] *Le Rêve* was worth more after it was torn and restored—$16 million dollars more!

What you have been through actually makes you more valuable. Think about it. The same art collector that didn't invest in the dream later invested $16 million more into it after it had been damaged and restored. Some of the same people that have written you off could be the very ones that end up believing in you the most.

God is in the business of restoration. He has not marked you out of His plan and His purpose just because you have been ripped, torn or broken by failure. He promises to restore to you the years that the swarming locust have eaten.[9] You may have messed up. You may have made a mistake. Maybe you made a bad business decision or a wrong call. You may think your failure will prevent you from uncovering your hidden potential and value. I want to tell you today that your failure is not final. You can be healed and restored through the power of Jesus Christ. God can still use you in this place.

As a pastor for more than thirty years, I have noticed an increase in people reaching places of hopelessness and despair. I have led and attended more funerals resulting from suicide within the last two years than in the entire time I have spent in ministry. The suicide rate is enormous and growing. Over the past twenty years, it has increased in nearly every state, with half of the states seeing a rise of more than 30 percent. Suicide is the tenth leading cause of death, the second among people ages 15 to 34.[10]

As I was writing this, I remembered two famous celebrities who took their own lives: iconic fashion designer Kate Spade, who founded a billion-dollar business, and celebrity chef, television personality and author Anthony Bourdain. We're talking about two successful and wealthy people who had everything you can imagine the world had to offer. And still they got to a place in their lives where they felt they had no hope. Heartbreaking!

Something is going on, and it's very real. People are losing hope for different reasons. It may have to do with an addiction, a career flop, severe depression, a crushed marriage, a relationship destroyed. Many times it has to do with failure. I think what sometimes happens is that people fall and make a mistake or a decision that brings about destruction in their lives, and they hit a place of hopelessness. Some people fall deep into sin, searching for what they think will make them happy, and end up broken inside. If this is your story, I want to tell you that *you might have gotten what you wanted, but you don't have to keep what you've got.* In Jesus, there is grace, forgiveness and restoration. Your failure does not have to be final. You can be restored in the place of brokenness.

I am terribly thankful that the Bible tells us stories about people not just because of their heroic acts, their righteousness, their goodness and their love for God. It also shows us their tremendous failures. It tells the whole story. I cannot relate to someone who is strong all the time, but I can relate to people who have both strengths and weaknesses. Abraham was the father of faith, but he also had a lying problem. Peter was bold and courageous, but he also had a temper. In fact, he got so ticked off one time, he cut off a man's ear. This reality is a powerful reminder that no matter how badly we have failed in our own lives, God meets us, where we are, in this place, with grace, mercy and forgiveness.

A Tattered Dream in the Right Hands

When I heard the story about *Le Rêve*, one of the first things I thought of is how important it is to put our shredded dreams into the right hands. When you fail, when you mess up, when you make a mistake, one of the greatest things you can do is put your failure into the nail-scarred hands of Jesus Christ.

Jesus knows how to restore. Notice the word *rest* in *restore*—it's important. Think of rest as a waiting period. It means that when God restores your torn dream, it will take time. It's going to take time to heal the torn marriage. It's going to take time to restore the life that's been devastated by drugs and alcohol. It's going to take time to let God heal you. But if you give Him that shredded place, He will restore you.

This is the very heart of Jesus—forgiveness. He is alive and well today, ready to restore you with a spirit of gentleness. Just when you think He ought to give it to you and judge you "real good," Jesus turns around and says, "I love you. I'm going to heal you. I'm going to restore you. I'm going to use you. And when I get through with you, your value is going to be greater than ever."

The enemy may have shredded and ripped your life to pieces, but Jesus says, "Come—I'll give you life more abundantly." Listen, Jesus is a safe place. There is nothing you have done or could do that His grace will not forgive and restore. Don't you give up because some kind of bad failure or hurt or heartbreaking situation has come into your life. You have a lot of living ahead of you. You have a lot of breakthroughs ahead of you. You have a lot of victories ahead of you, if you'll only let God restore what the enemy has torn to pieces. David sang, "Yet I am confident I will see the Lord's goodness while I am here in the land of the living" (see Psalm 27:13). God will send you His best!

Hard places lead to high places. God does not look for perfect places for you. He works in surprising places. So whether you are stuck in a famine or standing in the midst of a broken dream, stay faithful. It's time to conquer your unwillingness to make a commitment and stick with it. If you have worked fourteen jobs, attended twenty different churches and gone from relationship to relationship, let me ask you some questions. When are you going to stand? When are you going to let God plant you permanently? When are you going to stay until you start bearing fruit? Then and only then will you have happiness and fulfillment.

Stay connected. Stay long enough to allow God to help you face your giants, conquer your mountains and reap acres of diamonds in your own field.

4

Open My Eyes

A visionary sees things that are not as though they are. As Hebrews 11:13 says, "These all died in faith, not having received the promises, but having seen them afar off were assured of them, embraced them." Vision will give you strength to persevere through tough times.

Your vision is your victory!

Jan Cooley's first real job was on the inspection line in a poultry processing plant. After his first day, his mom asked how it went.

"I don't think I like it too much," fifteen-year-old Jan replied, "but I think I'll stay for the summer."

Coming from a hardworking family who lived in a cotton mill village, this teenager knew the value of having a few extra bucks in his pocket. Throughout the next twenty-some years, Jan worked in the poultry business in a variety of positions. He loaded trucks, stocked in the cold storage area and eventually worked his way up to quality control manager at J. D. Jewell, Inc., the biggest poultry processing plant in the region. After Jan was terminated from one company for refusing to release precooked product that was undercooked, he started to think about working for himself. He dreamed of one day owning his own poultry business. Two decades later, when Jan was in his mid-forties, he launched out on his own on a wing and a prayer. Founded in 1987, Kings Delight quickly grew in size and profit. Over the next ten years, Jan absorbed a poultry processing company and expanded into five production facilities. In 2001, he employed more than 1,000 people, and sales exceeded $100 million throughout the world. Jan continued to build his poultry business, acquiring and selling various companies and venturing into other businesses along the way.

Vision will give you strength to persevere through tough times.

Jan is a trusted friend of mine. When he told me his story, I learned a few fascinating things about him and his entrepreneurial journey. The one that struck me most was how his eyes were always open to opportunity. Jan is gifted with foresight. From the start, he was able to look ahead and see what the next big thing could be. For instance, he started a thigh deboning plant where the deboning was done manually or by hand while other companies used a machine. His insight in trying a different method increased yields and quality and proved to be a pivotal point in his success. Not too many years after that, Jan had the foresight to take a risk and invest significant capital in creating a plant that processed fully cooked poultry products. Within the first summer of opening the plant, business soared, leading to bringing two more fully cooked poultry plants online.

From the beginning, Jan was hands-on in day-to-day operations. He never let anything go to waste. He walked through his plants every day, observing what was or was not getting the right yield, and he immediately took action to correct it. Many people would have overlooked or walked right by these inefficient practices, but not Jan. He paid attention to everything.

Jan attributes part of his success to the people who have worked for him. People are very important to him. His vision was not just to see the potential of his company. He saw potential in his employees. Instead of recruiting corporate heads from other companies to work for him, he saw diamonds in those who already worked for him. Jan raised up ordinary people to high positions. They became supervisors, managers and executives who helped him grow a successful international business. Others may have overlooked them, but Jan believed in them.

Jan and his wife, Betty, are some of the most philanthropic people I have ever known. They are givers to needy people in the community and in the city. They have received numerous awards for their benevolence. They have also been extravagant givers to our church, helping us with every building project in our ministry that has been used to reach a multitude of souls. Jan will be the first one to tell you that God has opened his eyes to see the diamonds no one else could see. What others were willing to waste or overlook became gold for reaching souls and building the Kingdom of God.

King David prayed, "Open my eyes, that I may see wondrous things from Your law" (Psalm 119:18). This prayer is foundational as we navigate through life. This is especially critical when you are walking through the fire and the pressure. God can open your eyes and see potential, beauty, truth and life where others cannot. It may not look possible in the natural, but if you ask, He can reveal to you acres of diamonds that you cannot see.

When the king of Syria was going to war against Israel, he surrounded the city where the prophet Elisha was staying with thousands of armed soldiers, horses and chariots. When Elisha's servant woke up in the morning, he walked out of his house to a frightening scene: The enemy had come to kill Elisha and him. In a panic, the servant ran back inside. With fear in his eyes he cried, "Alas, my master, what are we going to do?"

Elisha was unmoved. "Don't be afraid," he said to his servant. "Those who are with us are more than those who are with them."[1] And then he prayed for God to *open the eyes of his servant* so he could see for himself.

I want you to take a moment while you're reading this book and place one of your hands on your eyes and say, "Holy Spirit, open my eyes." Be open to receiving vision from Him.

When God opened the eyes of Elisha's servant, the young man saw the horses and chariots of fire covering the mountain around Elisha. God's army! When God opens your eyes, you can see provision. When God opens your eyes, you can see the right direction. When God opens your eyes, you can see protection that the unseeing eye cannot see. If you ask God to open your eyes, you can see chariots of fire around your family, around your marriage, around your sickness, around your disease, around your depression, around your anxiety. When you didn't think He cared, when you didn't think He understood, when you didn't think He was moving, you will see that God was there all the while.

God can also open your eyes to what you have right now, even in a place that looks desolate. Proverbs 17:24 offers great insight on how we can do our part in uncovering God's best in our lives: "Wisdom is in the sight of him who has understanding, but the eyes of a fool are on the ends of the earth."

In other words, when you are a wise person, you begin to see and appreciate what's around you. You begin to see and appreciate the people in your life, like your family. You begin to see and appreciate the things that you have, like your job. You begin to appreciate the place God has called you to, even though it's not quite what you expected.

And the fool? His eyes are on the ends of the earth, everywhere else but right here, right now. He is thinking, *If I had this. If I had that. If I could go over here. If I could go over there. If I had that man and not this man. If I had that woman and not this woman. If I had his job or her talent, or if I could only catch a big break.* Fools don't appreciate what they have.

Wise people learn to value what God gives them. They stay rooted. They get disciplined. They stay planted. They remain where God has called them to until He tells them to move. Wise people see opportunity where there is devastation. Life in the midst of a drought. Dreams in place of brokenness. The wise person values what he or she has. *Don't overlook the potential of where you are.* When you are in the land God has called you to, everything you dream of is right there, if you would just sow into it.

> *When you are a wise person, you begin to see and appreciate what's around you. You begin to see and appreciate the people in your life, like your family. You begin to see and appreciate the things that you have, like your job.*

The first step in beginning to see the treasure in who you are and where you are is to look into the mirror of God's Word. It shows you who you really are and who you are going to be.

Occasionally I find myself looking into a natural mirror, and Satan will point out everything wrong with me. "You should be doing so much for God. You're not good enough. You're a piece of trash. You're not a good father. You're not a good husband. You're not a good preacher. You'll never amount to anything." This may shock you, but I hear that voice. And I've learned the only way to overcome these thoughts of hopelessness and dark depression is to keep looking into the right mirror.

Look Into the Right Mirror

Marina Chapman's first memory was playing in her backyard as a five-year-old. The next thing she remembered was a dark hand covering her mouth with a white cloth. She remembers being tossed into a truck and driven deep into the jungles of Colombia.

Her captors abandoned her in the jungle, and Marina was all alone. When night set in, she crawled under a bush. The eerie night sounds of the jungle echoed around her. Imagine the sheer terror this young girl must have felt. Tears, trembling, whimpering in fear, calling out for a mother who never came.

The next day Marina walked for hours, looking for signs of human life. Nobody came. Night fell again, and Marina curled up in a tight ball, trying hard to ignore the sounds of branches snapping and the rustle of foliage. Exhausted, brokenhearted, thirsty and famished, Marina fell asleep. When she awoke, she was surrounded by monkeys. Big ones. Little ones. Old ones and young ones. Suddenly, one of the bigger ones stepped away from the circle and approached her. Marina was petrified. When this monkey got close enough, he stretched out his arm and swatted her on her side. Another monkey did the same and then began to dig his fingers into the little girl's hair and over her face. The smaller monkeys got curious and started probing and poking Marina, making wild, terrifying noises.

"Get off me!" Marina yelled, and eventually the monkeys lost interest in her. But Marina began to watch them, following them around. She saw them eat nuts and berries. She watched them drink water out of giant leaves. Monkey see, monkey do. The monkeys got used to her and allowed her to sit in the trees with them. She even found a nook in a tree and slept there with them. Finally, they fully accepted her into their family.

Days turned into weeks. Weeks into months. Months into years. No human contact or verbal communication. No clothes and no school. Not even a glimpse of a human being. Living with the monkeys was her life now. And Marina began to get comfortable in what most of us would consider hell. She began to walk on all fours. She climbed trees. She forgot how to speak her language and learned how to communicate like the monkeys.

One day, everything changed. Sitting in a tree, Marina noticed something shiny on the jungle floor. She came down from the tree to retrieve it. She played with the strange object for a while, turning it around in her small hand. Then she got the shock of her life—it was alive! Two eyes stared back at her, with a nose and a mouth. It looked like a wild animal. She had never before seen anything like it. Frightened, Marina threw the object down and ran away.

But she was still curious, and later she retrieved the object and looked at it again. Then it hit her. The object wasn't alive. It wasn't a wild animal looking back at her. It was a mirror reflecting an image, a face. Her face.

For the first time Marina could remember, she had a glimpse of who she was. She was not like the monkeys. She was not born to be what they are. She did not know exactly who or what she was, but now she knew what she was not. As Marina put it, "I had forgotten I was human, and now I'd been reminded."[2]

This awareness of who she was—or wasn't—changed everything. After five years in the jungle, Marina was discovered by hunters. She had some hard years after that before being rescued by a family in Bogotá, Colombia, who sent her with other vulnerable children to England, where they could be safe. There she eventually got married and had two children. Today, Marina is almost seventy years old. One of her favorite pastimes is climbing trees and grooming her granddaughter's hair.

This incredible woman had only to look into a mirror to see what she was, what she was not and what she could become.

Life may tell you that you are an addict, a failure, a loser, not smart enough, not pretty enough or not good enough. But if you look at the Word of God, you will see that you are forgiven. You will see that you are the head and not the tail.[3] You will see a God who has a purpose for your life. Someone may have told you that you're good for nothing, but your heavenly Father says you are a royal diadem in the hand of the living God.[4]

You were not born to be an addict. You were not born to live in condemnation and guilt because you're all messed up. You are created in the image of the living God, and He said you are beautifully and wonderfully made.[5] Acres of diamonds!

No matter how unworthy you may feel about yourself, by the blood of Christ and the power of the cross, He will bring you out of the jungle of depression, low self-esteem and worthlessness. And once you have seen who you really are in the mirror of God's Word, you will never be the same again. Your jungle experience will be ruined.

Ephesians 1:17–18 tells us,

That the God of our Lord Jesus Christ, the Father of glory, may give to you the spirit of wisdom and revelation in the knowledge of

Him, the eyes of your understanding being enlightened; that you may know what is the hope of His calling, what are the riches of the glory of His inheritance in the saints, and what is the exceeding greatness of His power toward us who believe, according to the working of His mighty power.

When you look into the mirror of Scripture, your eyes will be enlightened and you will see what God sees.

When God looks at you, He does not see just your failures. He does not see just your struggles. God superimposes His image in that heavenly mirror over what you presently are, and He sees Jesus. He sees everything you can be. When we continually read and hear the Word, it begins to change our concept of who we are. He is saying to us, "I'm changing you. If you are in Christ, you are a new creation. Old things have passed away; behold, all things have become new."[6]

You may think you are unworthy, that acres of diamonds could never exist in your life, in your home or wherever God has called you to be. I'm telling you today that you are the righteousness of God in Christ Jesus. You are a water walker. You are a mountain mover. You are a giant slayer. You are a child of the Most High God. That is who you are.

Get a Picture

Perhaps you have been clinging to promises God has spoken to you about the place where you currently are, but you're frustrated because they are not happening. It might be because you're not doing this one thing: You have to let the promise become a picture.

When we were planning to build our first building, we were thick in the initial stage for a while, meeting with architects and creating design plans. I had heard about a pretty new church in Charlotte, North Carolina, that was similar to what we wanted. I decided to go check it out.

When I saw it, I was mesmerized. The building was huge. The architecture was breathtaking, with glass on all sides. It was a beautiful church. Immediately I had a picture in my mind of our church with similar features. I remember standing on the stage of that church and looking out into the empty seats. I could just see those same seats in our church back in Gainesville, filled with people being impacted for and exalting Jesus. The vision of what our church would be was firmly established in my mind.

Before I left, I visited their media store and purchased a postcard of the building. I brought it back home with me and tucked it into the top drawer of my desk. Every day I would look at this postcard and imagine our church. Now, we had not even cleared the land yet, nor did we have all the money we needed to build. But I had the picture. And every day, I would take that postcard out of my desk and look at it, thinking about our own church we would one day have. When we started building and got slapped with some setbacks, I would glance at the picture to remind me of where we were going. When you know you are going to a better place and you focus your eyes on that picture, you can tolerate where you are because you know it is only temporary.

You can't get somewhere you can't see. You will not find acres of diamonds until you get a divinely inspired image of what they might look like. You might see where you are as a field of failure, a land of hurt, a home of bitter contention, a place of disaster. All bad things. You need to get a picture of and meditate on "whatever things are true, whatever things are noble, whatever things are just, whatever things are pure, whatever things are lovely, whatever things are of good report, if there is any virtue and if there is anything praiseworthy" (Philippians 4:8).

God has called you to where you are for a reason. There is a promise there. A purpose. It is time to start turning that into a picture, no matter what your life or your place looks like right now. Remember, pictures are developed in darkrooms.

See yourself loved. See yourself whole. See yourself prospering. See your family united. See your workplace peaceful. See yourself making a difference. See your kids serving God. See your spouse going to church with you. See yourself impacting your community. See yourself blessed. See yourself joyful. See yourself beating that addiction. This is what God sees for you. He is for you; who can be against you? Get that picture in your mind.

Your life will always move in the direction of the dominant image you create in your mind. So get a picture of the right things.

When Moses sent the twelve spies to check out the Promised Land, he asked them to bring back some fruit. It was as though he was saying, "I want to transform the promise into a picture." The spies brought back grapes the size of watermelons. What a picture! But the spies didn't capture that image. Instead, they came back talking about the size of the giants. That is the picture they focused on. They should have come back seeing the picture of the fertile land God had promised them. They should have been armed with confidence, knowing they could defeat the giants because God is bigger than giants.

The picture matters. This is biblical. God gave Abraham a promise, but He also gave him a vision. He said, "Abraham, I know you're an old man. And I know your wife thinks you had a senior moment when you told her she was going to get pregnant, but if you don't believe my promise, look up toward the heavens. Count the stars. So shall your descendants be.[7] When it gets dark, look up." God gave Abraham a nighttime vision. He gave the man a picture.

The picture matters.

See It and Believe It

Over and over in the Bible we see God give His children a picture, a dream, an illustration to help make His promises clear.

In Judges 7, God promised Gideon He would deliver the Midianites and Amalekites into his hands. On the surface, the paltry three-hundred-man army of Israel was greatly outnumbered, out-resourced, and out-planned by the 135,000 soldiers from Midian. Gideon wasn't confident. The promise wasn't enough for him.

God knew this. So he told Gideon, "If you don't believe me, go down to the enemy's camp with your servant, and you'll hear what they say. Then your hands shall be strengthened to fight."[8]

Gideon obeyed God's instruction. He hid at the edge of the enemy camp, watching and listening. He saw thousands and thousands of soldiers. Armed and dangerous. Ready for war. Not an encouraging picture to Gideon, I imagine. Then he heard one of the soldiers talking to his buddies about a disturbing dream he'd had. The guy was freaking out. "You're not going to believe this," he said in a panic to his fellow soldier. "A loaf of barley bread rolled down the hill and wiped us out! Can you believe it?"

His friend gasped as the color drained from his face. "That's not just a dream—I know exactly who that loaf of barley bread is! It's Gideon, the leader of the army of Israel. God has delivered Midian and the whole camp into his hands!"[9]

And upon hearing this—boom!—Gideon got a picture in his mind. He saw God's promise coming to pass. He saw victory. He saw God using him. He saw his acres of diamonds. After he got that image in his head, he started to worship.

A promise from God is a revelation of God's divine intentions in your life through Scripture. The key is to turn the promise into a picture. You will never possess the promises of God until you see them. If you see them, then God can bring them to pass. Before a promise or a prophecy will ever manifest, you have to picture it in your mind. If you see it, you can have it. If you see it, God can do it. If you see it, it can become a reality.

If you are struggling with addiction, get into the promises of God. The Word says you can be free. Your acres of diamonds is freedom. Start renewing your mind. Do not see yourself as a nobody. Do not see yourself as an addict. Do not see yourself as a failure. Get filled with what God says and create an image in your mind of walking in freedom.

Believing something is crucial, but so is seeing it. Without vision, the people perish (see Proverbs 29:18). In other words, if there is no vision for the future, there is no power in the present. The more vision you have for your future, the more power you have for your present.

I love what Jack Nicklaus, winner of eighteen major championships and arguably the greatest golfer of all time, said: "I never hit a shot, even in practice, without having a very sharp, in-focus picture of it in my head. It's like a color movie."[10] If your mind is persuaded by a picture, then your body begins to respond. Let a picture form in your mind of God's promise to you, and He will begin to develop it into reality.

I remember when God started calling me to preach. I didn't know what that would look like or how I would get there, but I could see it. I saw myself preaching on television. I saw the cameras before we had any money to buy them. I saw a church that was blessed and winning souls for Jesus. I saw myself winning. I saw myself overcoming.

I have been at Free Chapel for more than thirty years, but the church has been in existence for more than sixty-five years. The former pastor, Roy Wellborn, scheduled me to preach a revival there every year when I was a full-time evangelist. The last time I preached for Pastor Wellborn, I had been scheduled nine months in advance. Just prior to my visit, however, he became ill, was hospitalized and passed away. He died on Friday night; I was to preach that Sunday. You can imagine how inadequate I felt standing in the pulpit two days after his death—the pulpit this beloved man had faithfully filled for more than three decades. As soon as the morning's service ended, they rolled in the coffin and held Pastor Wellborn's memorial service.

At that time, I had no idea that I was there by the divine plan of almighty God. I am sure that when Pastor Wellborn scheduled me to preach in his church, he had no idea he would be in heaven that very week, or that God had already chosen me as his replacement.

But even when God led me to Free Chapel and I pulled up to preach at my first service, I had a picture inside of me that God had given for this church. I did not see that church struggling. I did not see that church half-empty. I did not see that church remaining small. God gave me more than a promise; He gave me a picture, and I saw it.

When I had been pastoring Free Chapel for a year or two and we were a few hundred people, we invited a guest speaker, Dr. Bob Harrison, to share a message. This man taught on having a miracle mentality. He used the story of Jesus calling Peter into the ministry. Peter had been fishing all night. When morning came, he had caught nothing. Jesus was about to tell Peter to follow

Him, but had He done that right then, what would have been the picture in Peter's mind? Empty nets. Jesus knew better. He didn't want Peter to have a small-minded view of saving souls. He wanted Peter to think big. And to do that, He needed to give him a picture. So Jesus told this soon-to-be disciple to throw his net over the other side of the boat. When Peter did, there were so many fish in the net, it started to burst at the seams.

Then Jesus told Peter to follow Him. "Don't be afraid! From now on you'll be fishing for people!" (Luke 5:10 NLT). At this critical juncture in Peter's life, he did not have a small picture in his mind of reaching a handful of people for Jesus. He had a miracle mentality, an image of overflow. Peter could see it, and He believed it.

When I heard this principle taught, it just clicked. It reinforced in me a mindset of full nets, not empty ones. And over time, God began to do this in our ministry. Thousands upon thousands of people came to faith in Jesus Christ. But I had to see it first.

Albert Einstein said, "Imagination is more important than knowledge. Knowledge is limited. Imagination encircles the world."[11] Knowledge is about facts. Imagination can take you beyond facts. That is what happened for the woman in the Bible with the issue of blood. Knowledge told her she had a blood disease, that she had spent all her money on doctors who could not help her, and that her situation was hopeless. Her imagination told her that if she could only touch the hem of Jesus' garment, if she could get a point of contact with the Healer, she would be well. This woman released her faith beyond facts. When this woman got a picture in her mind and followed through, she was healed.

Facts may tell you that you shouldn't believe. Facts may tell you that you can't build a successful business. Facts may tell you that the odds are stacked against you. Facts may tell you that you're not educated enough, that you don't have any connections, that you lack the support you need. But if you get a picture from God, you will get a vision for your future. And it is always more than enough.

Ask God for a picture of your acres of diamonds. Then, see it and believe it. Nothing is impossible with God. You have more potential than you think. You can achieve more than most expect of you. If you can see it, you can be it! Ask God to open your eyes to the potential of where you are right now.

5

Hell in the Hallway

've heard it said that when God shuts one door, He will open another. That is true, but sometimes it's hell out there in the hallway.

Sometimes when a door shuts, another door does not open instantly. You're standing in the hallway. You feel stuck in that place without instruction or direction. The problem with most of us is that we're too impatient when we are waiting in the in-between place. There is a work going on in you right where you are now. You may not be fully aware of it, but without it, you would never be qualified to handle what God has for you in the future.

Today, are you walking through the dark hall of divorce? Maybe you are going through the dark hall of economic disaster. The dark hall of depression. The dark hall of failure. The dark hall of disease and sickness. God is not through with you. I want to show you how you can walk through the hallway and not lose heart. When it seems impossible to see acres of diamonds, here is what you do in the in-between place:

- Remember the Lord is your doorkeeper.
- Thank God for doors that did not open.
- Make worship a priority.

Remember the Lord Is Your Doorkeeper

Scripture teaches us that God is our doorkeeper. "He who has the key of David, He who opens and no one shuts, and shuts and no one opens: I know your works. See, I have set before you an open door, and no one can shut it" (Revelation 3:7–8). God opens doors and He shuts doors.

When you are in the in-between place and you are trying to get to another place, there's this thing called a door. A door separates one room from another. This is important because it means that you don't have to go far to make the transition. Sometimes we think that we are going to stay in the hell of a hallway forever. But the truth is, even as you read this book, God can set a door in your life, and you can walk through the fire out of the hallway and into another place.

You can be in a place of sorrow one moment, and God can transition you through a door to a place of joy. You can be in a place of brokenness one moment, and God can transition you through a door to a place of wholeness. All it takes is a door. And with one step, you can access it and everything changes.

The Lord is your doorkeeper. Never forget this.

Open doors give you access to something. Closed doors deny you access. If you trust God as your doorkeeper, He is going to allow or deny you access to His plan and His purpose for your life.

When the children of Israel came out of Egyptian bondage, God parted the Red Sea so that they could walk through it on dry ground. God had opened a door. And when the water caved in and swallowed up the Egyptian army in pursuit of the Israelites, God closed it.

Sometimes we forget God is still God. He is mighty. He is strong. He is powerful. And He is in control. If He wants to shut a door, He can. If He wants to open a door, He can. All it takes is being in the right place at the right moment. Even when you are licked by flames in the hallway, remember who your doorkeeper is.

Life has doorkeepers. Some people can shut you out. They can stop you from having access to something or someone. They can make you feel like you do not belong. People may try to block your progress. People may try to stop you from pursuing what God has for your life. People may try to keep you from believing acres of diamonds exist, even in the trial. But they are no match for God. He can open a door no man can shut. I don't care who dislikes you or does not believe in you; if you're supposed to be somewhere, God will get you there. If you are asking Him to uncover acres of diamonds, know that He is your doorkeeper. Humankind is not in charge of your door out of the hallway. Nor is the devil in charge of the door.

The Lord is your doorkeeper.

When the angel rolled the stone away from the entry of Jesus' tomb, God opened the door to His resurrection and our joy. He opened a door no man could shut. If you surrender to God during your times of testing and trials, He will open the right doors and close the wrong ones.

I know the hallway can be hell. And when you are in it, there is a great temptation to give up. Remember the words of the apostle Paul:

Do not cast away your confidence, which has great reward. For you have need of endurance, so that after you have done the will

85

of God, you may receive the promise: "For yet a little while, and He who is coming will come and will not tarry. Now the just shall live by faith; but if anyone draws back, my soul has no pleasure in him." But we are not of those who draw back to perdition, but of those who believe to the saving of the soul.

Hebrews 10:35–39

God is with you in the hallway.

So do not quit. Do not give up. You are not defeated. You are not weak. Through the blood of Christ, you are strong. You are mighty. "Lift up your heads, O you gates! And be lifted up, you everlasting doors! And the King of glory shall come in. Who is this King of glory? The LORD strong and mighty, the LORD mighty in battle."[1] You are better off fighting a war alongside God than playing in Disneyland without Him.

Thank God for Doors That Didn't Open

I rejoice when God opens a door in my life. I have also learned to thank Him for the doors that didn't open.

When our daughter Connar was seventeen, she had a horrible scare when she was in California. One night after youth group, Connar picked up some clothes at the house and drove to a friend's, where she had planned to spend the night. By 10:00 p.m., most of Orange County is closed. So when Connar was stopped at a red light, all was quiet. The only other car around was right in front of her, stopped at the same red light. When the light turned green, the driver of that car accelerated for a few seconds but suddenly slammed on his brakes. Connar tried to stop in time, but she ended up hitting the car in the rear. As a newbie driver, having had her license for barely two weeks, my daughter started freaking out. It was her first accident in the car we had just purchased for her. Connar was terrified of having to tell Cherise and me that she had hit a car. Panic and tears set in.

The other driver signaled with his hand for her to pull into the parking lot next to the street. Connar did, still shaking and crying uncontrollably. The parking lot was empty. And dark. The driver, who looked to be in his late forties/early fifties, got out of the car. As our daughter tells it, he looked "normal" and started asking questions "like a typical father."

"Are you okay? This isn't your car, is it? Your parents are going to be real upset at how much damage you've done."

Then, he asked how old she was.

"Seventeen," Connar replied, blinking through tears, hands trembling.

The man paused for a second, then said, "Perfect."

Later on, his response in that moment haunted her. At the time, however, Connar did not sense any danger because she could not think straight. She was mostly upset about having gotten into an accident. The man continued to ask her questions for a few minutes. Slowly, Connar began to realize this was a very dangerous situation. With a swift glance at both cars, she finally assessed the damage. There was zero damage to her car, and his had a massive dent on the back. She knew she needed to get out of there—and fast.

Sitting in the passenger seat of her car, her legs out the open door, Connar fumbled in the glove compartment for her insurance information. In tears she handed the man the card and said, "Just copy this down, so I can go home."

The man looked at her and smirked. With one hand clamped on the open door, he said, "I don't want that."

"What do you want?" Connar asked, petrified.

"I think I'll just have sex with you in the back of this car and you won't tell anyone."

With horror, Connar whispered under her breath, "Oh . . . you are a pedophile."

He laughed in her face and said, "No one is going to believe you."

Connar remembered her mom telling her that if she was ever in this type of situation to go ballistic. *Yell, scream—and do it all at the top of your lungs.* That's exactly what our daughter did. And in a matter of ten seconds, still screaming, Connar slammed the passenger door shut, jumped into the driver's seat, locked the doors, and started honking the horn like crazy. My daughter says this was nothing less than a miracle. In that moment, she knew exactly what to do to keep the situation from taking a devastating turn. The man was stunned. He had not expected her to do that. She could hear him saying, "Calm down. Just calm down," through the open windows.

And then, with Connar still shrieking and the horn still blowing, the man ran back to his car and took off, driving through a red light on his way out of town. And that's when she called us and 9-1-1. Connar remembers the police officer who came to the scene saying this was a new way that sexual predators were getting their victims. "It's a miracle he didn't just knock you out," he told her. She also learned the massive dent on his car was from a previous incident in which he had tried the same thing with another girl.

I am beyond grateful that the plans the enemy had to destroy my daughter fell through. That night Cherise and I got on our knees and thanked God for what didn't happen. I know that not every story has a happy ending like ours. Sometimes in a broken world, terrible things happen to good people without any explanation from God. Bad things happen to us all, but I think one of the greatest lessons we can learn is to celebrate all the times in our lives when God protected and delivered us from things that didn't happen.

In the story of Esther, we learn about a feast begun to celebrate this very idea. God established seven feasts in the Old Testament so His people would always remember certain events in their history. Human beings have a tendency to forget. This was God's way of making sure the people of Israel always remembered what was most important.

Before I get to the story, I want to share a couple of interesting things about the Feast of Purim. First, it is not one of the original seven feasts, and it was not commanded by God. It was a divinely inspired feast authorized by King Ahasuerus.

The other interesting fact is that the book of Esther is the only book in the Bible in which God's name is never mentioned. You won't find one Hebrew name of His. Not Elohim, not Jehovah, nothing. And yet God's fingerprints are all over this record in Scripture. (Side note: Seasons will come in life when you have zero evidence to believe God is working, but when you look back on that time, you will discover He was there all along. Active behind the scenes. From the shadows. Undercover. God is always at work in your life.)

Here is a quick summary of the story.

The Jewish people were on the verge of destruction because of the evil conspiracy of Haman, one of King Ahasuerus's advisors. Haman hated Mordecai because he did not bow down to him. Instead of just killing him, however, Haman decided to kill every Jewish person in the kingdom. So Haman cast lots, similar to a lottery, to determine on what day this would happen. Once he established this date, Haman approached King Ahasuerus to make the genocide official. He got his permission, and a decree was sent to everyone in the kingdom, notifying that all Jews, young and old, men, women and children, were to be killed on the thirteenth day of the twelfth month.

You need to understand the significance of this. In the moment that Haman cast this "lot," he was officiating the worst day in the history of the people of Israel. On the thirteenth day of the twelfth month, the Jews would face annihilation. Do you see how precise the enemy's plan is? He operates the same way today.

Satan comes to steal, kill and destroy.[2] He hates you because you reflect Jesus Christ. And he sets up certain times and events to destroy you, to take your kids out, to cause your marriage to fall apart, to crush your dreams, to steal your joy, to kill your faith. Hell in the hallway.

The word *pur* means "lot," as in the casting of a lot. Purim, as in the Feast of Purim, is the plural of *pur* and means "lots." Evidently, the enemy had planned to do one thing on one day, but an unseen party was watching, and He said, "I know you cast your lot, devil, but I'm about to cast lots. And what I cast is going to overcome what you planned and strategized against My people."

Back to the story.

The people of Israel were about to be slaughtered. Eradicated. Butchered. Massacred. Wiped out. Mordecai sought help from Queen Esther, asking her to appeal to the king on behalf of the Jews. His request meant Esther would have to literally risk her life, for it was very dangerous to approach the king without being summoned first. Consequently, Esther called a fast. Those 72 hours of fasting changed the history of the world.

When Esther finally approached the king on behalf of her people, they became a nation not of defeat, annihilation, suffering and shame but of favor. Not only did the king abolish Haman's decree, he also bestowed upon the Jews honor and promotion.

The king allowed a holiday called the Feast of Purim to be established, which is honored in Israel still to this day, to celebrate this reversal—to celebrate what didn't happen. The Jewish people threw a big party. They ate. They drank. They danced. They exchanged gifts. What the devil had marked as a day of massacre, God turned into a time of gladness and joy.

God has a way of canceling the verdict of the enemy.

Celebrate what didn't happen.

The enemy may have planned for them a day of destruction, but God, through Queen Esther, determined for them a day of deliverance. God can turn your day of destruction into a day of deliverance.

We often talk about being grateful for what we have and the wonderful things that have happened to us, but when was the last time—if ever—you thanked God for what didn't happen? We ought to stop whatever we're doing and throw a party for the door that God didn't open. For the guy you didn't marry because years later he would have been a deadbeat. For the girlfriend who broke up with you because she would have gone back to her ex-boyfriend. For the job that didn't work out because you held out for the one God wanted you to have. For the business deal that went sour before it would have bankrupted you.

Often, when God shuts a door, it is for our protection. Am I ever glad the Lord is my doorkeeper and not me. I can't tell you how many doors I would have kicked in, thinking I was supposed to do something that in reality was not part of God's plan. If something doesn't work out after you have prayed about it, guess what? God just shut a door. Not to punish you or hurt you, but to protect you.

Like Esther, there are times in our lives when God protected and delivered us from things that didn't happen. He shut the door and locked it. He kept us safe. He said that no weapon formed against us shall prosper. It should have happened. It almost happened. But because of God's hand of protection, it didn't happen.

Hasn't God been good to you? Where would you be today without Him? Before you take a step forward today, take some time and give thanks to Him for all the things that could have happened, that should have happened, that almost happened, but because of His unseen hand of protection didn't happen. Think about an opportunity that didn't pan out for your good, or a situation that could have proved destructive but left you unscathed. Start celebrating all the doors that closed in your life.

When you are in the hallway, God can turn things around. You might not see Him. You may not feel Him. You may think He is not even there. But He is. The enemy may have cast one lot to destroy you, but God casts another lot in your favor. It just takes a door. Whatever it is you are facing, decide today to trust that He who began a good work in your life is faithful to complete it.

Make Worship a Priority

When the heat and pressure are turned up and it is hard to see the treasure in our lives, one of the most important things we can do is worship.

Thousands of years ago, Joshua stood before the towering walls of Jericho, the strongest city in the Promised Land. It was the first city that had to be conquered in order for the people of Israel to walk into their promise. God had given them the land, but they would have to fight for it.

Just before God delivered the city into the hands of the Israelites, an angel appeared to Joshua. "Take off your shoes," he told the leader of the people, "for where you are standing is holy ground."³ He might as well have said, "Joshua, take off your shoes and stay awhile. I know you're a busy leader. I know you're feeling the pressure. I know you've got a lot riding on you. I know the people are anxious, packed up and ready to go. I know they've been waiting a long time for this. But stop for a moment. First things first."

Joshua took off his shoes, fell on his face, and worshiped. I love this. A man in the hell of the hallway worships.

When you are pressed on all sides and feeling the heat from the fire, worship. You can't afford not to. It's not a waste of time. It's not a distraction. It's a posture of leaning on God. It's a means of looking to Him as your source. It's a way of maintaining a spirit of dependence on Him.

In Hebrew, the name Jabez means "sorrow,"⁴ or distress and grief. The very name reminds us that we cannot escape troubled times. Life will bring trials and tears in some shape or form. Jabez, mentioned only three times in the Bible, was from the tribe of Judah, and Judah means "praise." When the twelve tribes of Israel wandered in the desert, moving and taking new territory, God always commanded Judah to go first. The lesson is simple: Before you go out into a new place, praise first. Before you ever get into the promises of God, praise first. Praise your way to victory.

I have learned that no matter how great your pain, your hurt or your sorrow, you can come out in victory if you will worship and praise the living God. This is spiritual warfare. Look at how powerful the Bible paints this picture: "Judah, you are he whom your brothers shall praise; your hand shall be on the neck of your enemies" (Genesis 49:8). When you worship God in the hell of the hallway, you grab the enemy by his neck. You are not in a defensive position; you are on the offense. Powerful!

Jabez refused to allow his beginning to dictate his end. He refused to allow his family or his borders to keep him down. He prayed, "Oh, that You would bless me indeed, and enlarge my territory, that Your hand would be with me, and that You would keep me from evil, that I may not cause pain!"[5] God granted his request. This is a prayer God is waiting for you to pray. And He will answer it for you, also!

It is time to be a boundary crosser. Start believing God for more instead of settling for less. If you will get in His presence and leadership, He will show you things He wants you to see.

Psalm 150:6 says, "Let everything that has breath praise the LORD." This is not a suggestion. This is a command. It does not matter what denomination you come from. It does not matter if you have a reserved or a charismatic personality. It does not matter if you're the emotional type or not. You are created to praise and worship your heavenly Father. Put on the garment of praise. When you begin to lift high the name of the Lord, you begin to change. You become a victor, not a victim. You move into new territory. You leave behind the past and march into the Promised Land.

Worship puts life in the proper perspective. It helps us see who we are in relation to who God is. When we look beyond our earthly circumstances and praise our heavenly Father, we send the Spirit of the Lord before us. We declare our dependence on Him and make known His presence in our lives. In this, we change the atmosphere. When we worship, strongholds and addictions can be broken. Sin can no longer hold us captive. Ultimately, our worship prepares us for victory.[6]

There is much purpose in our worship. When we sing, God listens. He responds. Keep worshiping in the hall.

Look, you're going to spend more time in life waiting than you will receiving. So settle down and learn to wait well. Galatians

6:9 tells us, "And let us not grow weary while doing good, for in due season we shall reap if we do not lose heart." Due season is when God knows you are ready.

I know it's hard to see God bless others while you are forced to wait. You are being tested by the very promises He gave you. When you are in the in-between place, the hallway between a closed door and the next open door, the enemy will whisper, "What are you doing here? Why has God forsaken you?" Be encouraged. The hallway you are in is the birthplace of promise and the day of small beginnings. God has not changed His mind, so don't you do it, either. When He wants you in a certain place, nobody can keep you in a dark pit. Your dream is not in the hands of others, it is in God's hand. Remember this: The purposes of God will always overcome the plans of man.

> *The purposes of God will always overcome the plans of man.*

A Long Walk Can Be a Gift

I have always liked a story popularized by Norman Vincent Peale:

> On Christmas morning, one of the natives brought the missionary a seashell of lustrous beauty. When asked where he had discovered such an extraordinary shell, the native said he had walked many miles to a certain bay, the only spot where such shells could be found.
>
> "I think it was wonderful of you to travel so far to get this lovely gift for me," the teacher exclaimed.
>
> His eyes brightening, the native answered, "Long walk, part of gift."[7]

You will never appreciate the gift of acres of diamonds if you neglect the long walk down the hallway. A process is involved in its uncovering. Prayer. Fasting. Believing. Trials. Hardships. Tears. We like to celebrate the gift—the blessings we receive, the answers to prayer, the miracles, the healing—but God sees the long walk.

People often see me on a platform and think that my preaching in front of large crowds and on TV is ministry. But there is more to it than that. My ministry includes all I have done up until this time and continue to do. It's the years being a pastor's kid and learning about the church. It's a lifetime of living out my faith not in public, but in private. It's the fasting. It's the praying. It's the sleepless nights. It's the crying. It's the countless hours praying and studying the Word of God. It's the problems. It's the pressure. It's the issues. It's the hell in the hallway. These things are all part of the long walk of the blessings of the ministry we have today.

When I think about that baby born in Bethlehem, I am thinking about the greatest gift in the world. It was beautiful. It was God in skin. His name was Jesus. He journeyed from perfect heaven to dirty earth.

The long walk was part of the gift.

For thirty years, Jesus never preached a sermon. He never healed a person. He just lived a normal life in a blue-collar family so that he could identify with you and me.

The long walk was part of the gift.

When I picture Jesus hanging on the cross at Calvary, I think of the great gift of salvation and forgiveness. I also think of the long walk to and from Gethsemane, where He prayed so fervently that His sweat became like drops of blood. I think of the long walk to Pilate's courtyard, where Jesus was beaten. I think of the long walk down the Via Dolorosa, as He struggled beneath the cross he bore. Sometimes we look at Jesus and only see a gift. We must not forget the long walk. You cannot fully appreciate the gift unless you appreciate the long walk that it took to bring the gift to you.

It's not enough to get out of the hallway. It's not enough to uncover acres of diamonds. It's not enough to have a gift. You've got to walk the walk. You've got to live the life. The walk down the hell in every hallway is a part of our gift.

God is looking for faithfulness in the long walk, fruit that we are being continually changed, transformed, purified and made in His image. This is what makes a gift worth it. You do not have to do anything to impress God other than to be faithful. As you ask God to open your eyes to the hidden potential of your life, walk with Him. Obey Him. Be faithful in the small things. Everybody walks. Nobody rides. Keep trusting God no matter how hot or how dark your hallway.

The Lord is your doorkeeper. In His timing, the hell in the hallway will turn to joy in the morning. When God has you in a holding pattern, while you are waiting for better to come to pass, don't become so intent on reaching your goals that you don't enjoy the things at hand. You will miss a lot trying to give birth outside of God's timing. Learn to enjoy where you are while you are waiting to get where you want to be.

❖ 6 ❖

Let It Take You Up

God wants you to understand that your life is like a field. The way He is going to pull the diamonds out of you is by cultivating your soil. The biggest changes do not happen above ground, at least not at first. The work begins underneath.

It's Gonna Get Windy

On September 26, 1991, in Oracle, Arizona, eight scientists entered an airtight, three-acre miniworld called Biosphere 2 in an experiment straight out of a science-fiction movie. This $150 million facility designed to mimic the earth's environment was pored over and analyzed by the "explorers" living within its walls. Housed in the self-contained bubble were a miniature rain forest, a desert, an ocean, a mangrove swamp, a savanna and a small farm. The scientists grew their own food, recycled their sewage and water, managed their air supply, inspected the ecosystems' health, collected data, studied, researched and wrote. One driving purpose of this two-year experiment was to see if humans could create

99

and survive in self-sustaining colonies in outer space. Though many lessons were learned from it, Biosphere 2 ultimately failed for a number of reasons. The one that struck me the most was the necessity of wind. I'll explain.

The trees in Biosphere 2 were growing faster than they would have in their normal environment on earth. Problem was, they would collapse before they could fully mature. The reason for this was the absence of wind in the dome. When plants and trees grow in the wild, wind keeps them moving, which helps create in trees what is called "stress wood." Stress wood helps trees grow in ways that absorb more sunlight and develop solidly to maturation. Without stress wood, a tree will grow fast, but it will not be able to support itself through the wear and tear that comes with a natural and sometimes severe environment. Wind is actually essential to the plant's growth and sustenance.

There's a great lesson here. Like it or not, weathering the storms of life builds our strength. Sometimes storms bring pain, but God is no sadist. He does not enjoy seeing you hurt, discouraged or struggling. Rather, He knows there is always purpose in the storm: to build your faith, your confidence, your praise, your prayer life and your dependence upon God.

It's in the dark places that God does His greatest work.

The cold does this same thing. During the winter season, when trees are barren, they are still very much alive. Similar to hibernation, they go through a process called dormancy. This is a means of self-preservation that keeps them alive during the winter. Without it, the buds from the previous summer will not blossom.

The peach tree is a good example. Did you know that it takes up to 1,000 hours of cold weather for a peach tree to grow peaches? The reason peach trees grow in Georgia but not in other states is because we have just enough warm days and cold days. Without a period of cold, you won't find a peach tree with peaches on it. If you want to bear fruit, you're going to need some cold days. It is not enough to live blessing upon blessing upon blessing, which is why God allows you to endure the cold. Out of these cold days, if we allow God to work His work in our fields, we will bear fruit.

If you want to grow and uncover your acres of diamonds, it will usually happen when the winds blow and the storm comes. I can't explain it. I don't understand it. But I have learned that it's in the dark places that God does His greatest work.

What Happens *in* You, Not What Happens *to* You

Shannen Wehunt never could have imagined that at 49 years old, she and her husband, J.T., would have already buried their only two children four years apart.

On November 12, 2012, Shannen and J.T.'s twelve-year-old son, Klate, was diagnosed with Marfan syndrome. It is a genetic disorder that affects the body's connective tissue, commonly in the heart and blood vessels. In April 2014 Klate underwent open heart surgery to repair his aorta. The walls of his aorta had dilated, which put him at risk for a life-threatening rupture. Surgeons worked furiously to fix it but were unsuccessful.

Shannen vividly remembers being taken with her husband and daughter to a small, private room in the hospital, where Klate's doctor told them, "I'm sorry, there is nothing more we can do." Klate was put on life support. Believing in God's mighty hand, Shannen had faith that He could heal her son. And God did, but not in the way she expected.

Shannen calls the next three days of her son's life a gift. "God gave us a minute to process what was happening with Klate," she told me. "He extended to us grace and gave us three days with our boy before he was taken to heaven." When Klate took his final breath on earth, Shannen remembers lying with her son in his hospital bed, tears pouring down her face. "As broken as I was, there was no greater gift than knowing that I had raised godly children. Klate knew the Lord. My son was healed in heaven. He has a new body, and I know I will see him again."

When Shannen left the hospital that day, even as grief unraveled like a storm within her, she made a vow to herself and to God. "The one thing I promised myself was not to be angry at God for taking my son. I meant it. And I stuck with it. The pain was unbearable, but my heavenly Father got me through. I always taught my children to trust the Lord, even when life is bad. And now I had to live it out, especially to my daughter."

Fourteen months later, Klate's sister, Kre, began complaining of excruciating pain in her tailbone that radiated down her legs. Tests and scans followed. On November 12, 2015, exactly three years to the day that Klate was diagnosed with Marfan syndrome, Kre was diagnosed with osteosarcoma, a kind of bone cancer. Fifteen months after Klate had passed away, the family received this news in the same room where the doctor had told Shannen, J.T. and Kre that Klate wouldn't make it.

Kre's prognosis wasn't hopeful. The first prayer Shannen prayed for her daughter was, *Lord, you healed my boy, and he has a new body in heaven. Please heal Kre on this earth so she can stay with me and her daddy. I can't do this again. I won't live through it.*

Over the next seventeen months, Kre endured 27 rounds of chemo, underwent 5 surgeries, took 800 prescriptive pills, had 70 shots and spent 275 days in the hospital. "Kre's attitude throughout this time was unbelievable," her mother told me. "I've never seen such a faith in anyone in my entire life like I did in that child. She never complained. Not once. She read her Bible faithfully. She prayed continually. And she never stopped believing God would heal her. J.T. and I drew grace and beauty off of Kre. She was our inspiration."

Then, a miracle. The combination of treatments worked. On September 1, 2016—Klate's birthday—Kre was declared cancer free. She had beat this wretched disease.

Kre was always making videos and posting them on social media. Not so other people could feel sorry for her, but so she could uplift those going through a tough time. She once said,

I never thought I would come so far, and the whole reason is because of God. God is always there for you to call on. He is the one who will pull you through every season in your life. There is a season for everything. Some are good. Some are bad. Some are ugly. Don't be in such a rush to get past the hard seasons. He has put you in that season for a reason, to make you grow. His timing is always perfect, so you have to trust that and trust in Him. Brighter and better days are ahead.

In a journal Shannen recently found, Kre had written,

Jeremiah 29:11, "For I know the plans I have for you, says the Lord, plans to prosper you and not harm you. Plans to give you hope and a future." That's proof right there that God's got you . . . when you find yourself in a dark season and you feel completely trapped and alone, just know that there are other broken people around you.

Toward the end of 2017, Kre found herself in terrible pain again. She had two nerve block procedures, which didn't help. In January 2018, devastating news: The cancer had returned. This time the osteosarcoma was on the right side of Kre's lower back and hip area. More chemo. More pain management. More pain. More tears. More fight.

This time, none of the treatment plans worked. The tumor kept growing. Kre was in so much pain that she had to lie on her left side, in the same position, for 52 days straight. The slightest movement proved agonizing. Still, Kre believed she would get better. That God would heal her. That she would beat cancer a second time. She kept smiling. She kept encouraging others. She kept her faith strong, praying and praising God every day, even when she could barely move. I love what she said once: "It never gets easier. It just gets better."

When I visited Kre in the hospital, Shannen told me something that has stuck with me since. "I still believe God will heal Kre, but either way this goes, I win. I won with my son. I will win with my daughter. And I'm going to win in the end. I don't feel like a winner in my flesh, but in my spirit I know I am." Her children loved God and had an eternal hope. This is victory!

Kre battled cancer for two years and eight months. On August 26, 2018, on a beautiful Sunday morning, this brave and faith-filled young lady ran into the arms of Jesus and into the presence of her brother Klate. Shannen and J.T. buried Kre the same day they celebrated Klate's birthday.

Kre had fought the good fight. She had kept the faith. During her life on earth, Kre spread her warmth and shined a light in the darkness, bringing hope and encouragement to those around her. She was 23 years old.

Life hurts for Shannen and J.T. "I miss my kids terribly," Shannen told me. "There are times I drive past Yellow Creek Cemetery, where both of my children are buried, and I just cry and cry. But I keep trusting the Lord. I keep reminding myself He is good. I keep thanking Him for giving me the gift of two beautiful children who are now in His arms.

"I can't say I understand this. But I choose to trust the Lord, even when it's painful. Even when it's lonely. Even when I know I will never hear my kids call me 'Mama' on this earth. I trust God. He's all I've got."

Shannen and J.T. are some of the most remarkable people I have ever met in my life. Their faith in God throughout the darkest moments in their lives is inspiring. I do not even pretend to imagine I know what they are going through. But I am very grateful for their example of unwavering faith. I don't know how they do it, but I applaud them for making the choice not to be angry, not to get bitter, not to let the enemy destroy them through their grief. Their road is painful, no doubt, but I know that what may have been planned for evil, in some way, God will use for good.

You cannot choose everything that happens to you in life, but that's not what matters most. It's not what happens *to* you, it's what happens *in* you that makes the difference.

> *It's not what happens to you, it's what happens in you that makes the difference.*

I am not a botanist, but years ago I learned something about plants that fascinated me. A type of plant tissue called meristem is the key to how plants grow and repair damaged cells. These undifferentiated cells have the ability to divide indefinitely and eventually differentiate. What does this mean? The meristem determines whether a plant develops new stems, leaves, flowers or roots. You can say that the function of meristem is making choices from what it has been given.

Picture with me an imaginary line running through a young plant. At some point in this line, a decision takes place. The meristem decides what would work well as a root or a shoot or a flower and then makes it happen.

While we aren't plants, we all have a spiritual meristem. We are going to do something with the trials that come our way. We can allow them to take us up or take us down. Isaiah 37:31 says, "And the remnant who have escaped of the house of Judah shall again take root downward, and bear fruit upward." Before you can grow to your full potential and achieve the heights God has planned for you, you must be firmly planted and rooted in faith. I pray that whatever you are facing today helps you dig deep roots and causes you to bear fruit upward.

Dig Deep Roots

What happens underneath the surface of our lives determines what happens above the ground. If your root system is going downward, it is only a matter of time before your fruit system starts bearing fruit upward.

Did you know that any tree, and even many plants, can be dwarfed to create a bonsai tree? Bonsai is a Japanese art form in which specific techniques are used to create small trees in containers that look like full-size trees. With the right tools and the right skills, you can take, say, a pine tree and prune its branches and trim its roots and turn it into a bonsai. While a pine tree can grow up to 150 feet tall, clip and trim it enough and it will remain a miniature version of itself. The tree will never reach its full potential. In Japan, you will find bonsai trees hundreds of years old that are only knee high.

This tells me something. There are people who have been coming to church a long time but remain bonsai Christians. They get offended easily. They cuss out someone who says something they don't like. They don't talk to people who treat them wrong. They don't have a rich prayer life. They don't give. They don't serve. They are born again, but their only claim to the Kingdom is fire insurance. They don't bear any fruits of the Spirit.

John the Baptist said, "And even now the ax is laid to the root of the trees. Therefore every tree which does not bear good fruit is cut down and thrown into the fire."[1] Jesus, too, had something to say about a fruitless tree:

> A certain man had a fig tree planted in his vineyard, and he came seeking fruit on it and found none. Then he said to the keeper of his vineyard, "Look, for three years I have come seeking fruit on this fig tree and find none. Cut it down; why does it use up the ground?" But he answered and said to him, "Sir, let it alone this year also, until I dig around it and fertilize it. And if it bears fruit, well. But if not, after that you can cut it down."
>
> Luke 13:6–9

Jesus said to give the tree a chance by fertilizing it, but if it still does not produce fruit, it should be cut down. What happens to a tree that does not produce? It's either cut down or thrown into the fire!

Bonsai Christians may go to heaven one day, but they never grow in this life on earth. They never get bigger. They remain dwarfed because they allow Satan to trim their roots over and over and keep them where they are. They never get into their own walk and rhythm with God. They are not fulfilling the purpose God has for their lives.

This might speak of your marriage. When you first married your spouse, I imagine you two were really close. You loved each other. You doted on each other. But ten or twenty years later, things look different. The relationship has stopped growing. Something happened along the way that stunted your marriage. This is where the enemy thrives. Over time, he comes alongside you with the shears of lies, contention, strife, bitterness, anger, resentment and entitlement. And he starts cutting away at the roots of your marriage, one moment, one conversation at a time.

He's so selfish. Snip.

I can't believe she did that again. Snip.

I can't take it anymore. I can do better. Snip.

Why did he say that? He must not love me. Snip.

I wonder if my ex is on Facebook. Snip.

Snip. Snip. Snip. Before you know it, what should be a flourishing relationship, what should be stronger than ever, is falling apart. The roots that should have grown deep are barely long enough to settle underneath the ground. Nothing but a bonsai tree.

This could also speak of your relationship with God. You got born again—and I am glad you did! But this is not the end of your Christian walk. Jesus did not bleed and die so that you could be saved without ever producing fruit or growing deep roots of prayer, deep roots of studying the Scriptures, deep roots of gathering with others, deep roots of sharing the Good News with others, deep roots of living a life for Jesus outside of two hours on a Sunday morning.

The secret to a tall, flourishing tree is the unseen roots.

In Isaiah 37:31, God was saying to Judah, "You are going to go through something. And when life gives you trouble and trials, you can either let it shatter your world or you can let your roots go deep so they take you up to bear fruit." This wasn't God's decision. It was Judah's. Just like it's yours today.

The devil's got an arsenal of shears and pruning tools. And if he can cut you off from your roots, he will stop you from growing and bearing fruit upward. Whatever life sends you, when something happens that you were not planning, you have to make a decision at your spiritual meristem line, somewhere deep inside of your soul. Say, "This is not going to take me down. I'm going to go through it. God allowed this to happen, and I am going to let the Holy Spirit take it and produce in me, through the cold days, fruit that I can't get any other way."

Jesus told a parable about a sower:

The sower sows the word. And these are the ones by the wayside where the word is sown. When they hear, Satan comes immediately and takes away the word that was sown in their hearts. These likewise are the ones sown on stony ground who, when they hear the word, immediately receive it with gladness; and they have no root in themselves, and so endure only for a time. Afterward, when tribulation or persecution arises for the word's sake, immediately they stumble. Now these are the ones sown among thorns; they are the ones who hear the word, and the cares of this world, the deceitfulness of riches, and the desires for other things entering in choke the word, and it becomes unfruitful. But these are the ones sown on good ground, those who hear the word, accept it, and bear fruit: some thirtyfold, some sixty, and some a hundred.

Mark 4:14–20

There are two types of bonsai Christians in this passage. There are those who receive the seed of the Word, but without deep roots they only endure for a time. When the hurricane of opposition tears through their lives, they crack and break. They produce little, if any, fruit. Some seed gets thrown in the thorns. This other type of bonsai Christian is so preoccupied with the cares of this world that the misdirected focus chokes the Word and they, too, become unfruitful.

Then we have the seed with deep roots. One of our goals as Christians is to become like this seed. These people hear the Word. They accept the Word. And they bear fruit. Tons of fruit. They take whatever life hits them with and allow God to use their circumstances to grow deep roots in Him and bear fruit upward.

If you will let it, the challenging situation you are in right now can take you up. Instead of getting hateful and cynical, you can let it produce in you the fruits of the Spirit: "love, joy, peace, longsuffering, kindness, goodness, faithfulness, gentleness, self-control."[2] God will not let you go through the trials of this life without gain. Out of that hardship, if you make the right choice, fruit will come.

Attitude Is Everything

In moments of great difficulty, your attitude is everything. You can gain or lose the victory according to your attitude.

There is a place in our soul, our spiritual meristem, that will produce either the root of bitterness or the fruits of the Spirit. The same sun that melts butter hardens clay. We can take what we get in life and toughen our spirits by getting offended, angry and acting like a victim. Or, through what comes our way, we can soften our spirits as we bear the fruits of love, joy, peace, kindness, gentleness, patience and long-suffering.

Paul knew what it was like to endure hardship. He also knew how to keep a right attitude in the thick of it: "For our light affliction, which is but for a moment, is working for us a far more exceeding and eternal weight of glory" (2 Corinthians 4:17).

Having the right attitude isn't always a natural reaction. It's a choice. It's a choice Shannen made when her son went to heaven. And it's a choice she made again when her daughter passed. When you are going through bad times, your goal should be to keep a good attitude. You would not choose the trial you're in, but that is what life is giving you, and God is allowing it. So you have to make a decision at the spiritual meristem in your soul to choose the right attitude. God will not do it for you. But He can help you through it.

Paul wrote about how a root of bitterness begins to grow. When it rises up, it can cause trouble. It can defile many. I cannot guarantee what will come your way, but I can guarantee you will have a thousand opportunities to get bitter in life. Somebody will hurt you. Some injustice will take place. Some disappointment will crop up.

Whether you get bitter at people or bitter at God, it is easy to let a root of bitterness take you down. Are you going to let a tough time become a bad cell in your soul? Or are you going to make the choice to turn it into a good heart cell? You decide how your spiritual cells activate and grow (or not). Choose not to let those situations grow a root of bitterness deep in your soul.

When you are tempted to allow bitterness to take up space, be intentional. Pray aloud, "God, I know what was sent could make me bitter, but today I choose to trust You. I choose not to get bitter. I'm going to let this trial transform into a blessing. I'm going to let what I'm groaning about make me grow. I'm not going to let adversity stop me. I'm going to let it advance me, and I'm going to bear fruit upward, because I make this decision."

Paul wrote,

That Christ may dwell in your hearts through faith; that you, being rooted and grounded in love, may be able to comprehend with all the saints what is the width and length and depth and height—to know the love of Christ which passes knowledge; that you may be filled with all the fullness of God.

Now to Him who is able to do exceedingly abundantly above all that we ask or think, according to the power that works in us, to Him be glory in the church by Christ Jesus to all generations, forever and ever.

Ephesians 3:17–21

When Paul talks about the "depth" of God's love, he's talking about the man or woman who has planted deep roots in God. And when he talks about the exceeding and abundant power of Jesus, it's not just for anybody. It's for the people who take what they're given and get better, not bitter.

I wish you hadn't gotten that bad report from the doctor. I wish you didn't have that turmoil in your marriage. I wish you hadn't lost your job. I wish you hadn't lost your business. I wish you hadn't lost your loved one. I wish you weren't struggling with whatever your family is going through right now. But I have a question for you: Are you going to grow roots of bitterness, or are you going to allow God to form in you character like Jesus' and bear fruit for His Kingdom? Your answer will determine your destiny. The right decision will allow you to uncover acres of diamonds in the fields of your trials.

What you are going through right now will either take you up or take you down. God's word to you today is that you will not grow if you allow the enemy to do what he wants to do through your darkest moments. But when you submit to God and say, "Lord, I'm Yours," and choose to have the right attitude, here's what happens:

> The righteous shall flourish like a palm tree,
> He shall grow like a cedar in Lebanon.
> Those who are planted in the house of the LORD
> Shall flourish in the courts of our God.

They shall still bear fruit in old age;
They shall be fresh and flourishing,
To declare that the LORD is upright;
He is my rock, and there is no unrighteousness in Him.[3]

You will not be moved. You will be fresh and flourishing. You will bear fruit upward.

Don't get offended at people or at God. Don't get bitter. Don't get angry. Don't get vengeful. Let the difficulty develop you. Let it make you stronger in Christ. How you choose to respond will make the biggest difference in your life. Don't let Satan stunt your spiritual growth by clipping your roots in times of trial. Pray. Seek God. Read the Word. Gather with others. Praise. Worship. The deeper your roots, the higher your fruit.

God's exceeding power is waiting on the decision that you make in your spiritual meristem. When you decide with the right attitude that what you are going through is not going to take you down, you will not grow roots of rejection, offense and bitterness. You are going to bear fruit, more fruit than you can ever imagine. This is God at work in your field. If you're going through one of your darkest seasons, remember what Shannen said. Remember the work of Jesus on the cross. Darkness does not have the final say. Death does not have the final word.

Ultimately, we win.

7

Let Down Your Bucket

In 1895, Booker T. Washington delivered a speech in which he told a powerful story of a ship lost at sea for many days.[1] The sailors on board this distressed vessel were without hope, exhausted from hunger and dehydrated to the point of death. Finally, someone spotted a boat far away. A signal was sent from the lost ship: "Water, water. We die of thirst."

The other ship signaled back, "Cast your bucket where you are."

The sailors were confused. Their signal was obviously being misinterpreted. They tried again. "Water, send us water." The same response was delivered: "Cast your bucket where you are." The dehydrated men were beside themselves with frustration. "We're going to die of thirst because these people don't understand what we're trying to say!" Desperate, they signaled again. Same response. Then, a fourth and final time. Same response.

Finally, the captain of the lost ship said, "I don't understand what it means, but we'll die if we don't try." He took a bucket and let it down into the ocean. When he brought it up, the captain couldn't believe his eyes. The bucket was filled with sparkling freshwater! What he did not know was that he was very near the mouth of the Amazon River, which deposits freshwater far into the ocean. All that these sailors had needed all along was right under them. Their thirst was satisfied.

Are you dry and thirsty? Do you desperately need life? You don't have to seek comfort or satisfaction in another person. You don't have to chase after another diamond. You don't have to try whatever the world says can fix your problem. Right here, where you are, is a well of living water. His name is Jesus Christ. If you will just let down your bucket, you will find acres of diamonds in Him. Everything you need, every provision for your body, soul and spirit, is in Jesus.

Do you need joy? Do you need hope? Do you need faith? Do you need peace? Do you need a future? Let down your bucket.

Undiscovered potential lies right before you. Even in your darkest hour, you can have living water in Jesus Christ. The key to finding this diamond is to get anchored in Him.

Get Anchored Right

In order for us to stay where God has called us, we have to get anchored right where we are. If you are not properly anchored, you will drift too much. I want to tell you a story you will never forget.

Early on February 28, 2009, Oakland Raiders linebacker Marquis Cooper, NFL defensive lineman and free agent Corey Smith, and former University of South Florida players William Bleakley and Nick Schuyler went fishing in the Gulf of Mexico. They sailed out to sea on a beautiful day and spent the next few hours having a good time. They talked. They laughed. They joked. They fished. In the late afternoon, the sunny and calm weather dissipated.

The cold swept in and the wind blew hard; no doubt a storm was coming. When Marquis made the decision to head back, the men discovered the anchor was stuck. They tried to pull it loose, but nothing worked. Someone suggested tying the anchor to the back of the boat and gunning the motor to pull it free. That didn't work either. In fact, it only made the situation worse, as the boat flipped over and capsized. Two days later, when the boat was found, Nick Schuyler was the only survivor. The agency that investigated the accident concluded the boating tragedy occurred as a result of "a mistake in anchoring."[2]

The mistake in anchoring made by these athletes ended in tragedy. There is a spiritual lesson for us as well. It is easy to get anchored to the wrong things in life. Busy schedules. Material success. Reputation. Drugs. Alcohol. Food. Pornography. Money. Fame. Ungodly relationships. The problem is, when the storms of life blow, none of these things will bring you peace. Or joy. Or rest. Or hope.

Only the right anchor will keep you from drifting away from the very place—the marriage, the community, the church, the relationship, the job—in which God has called you to stay.

Hebrews 6:17–20 is an amazing passage that offers us an incredible promise:

Thus God, determining to show more abundantly to the heirs of promise the immutability of His counsel, confirmed it by an oath, that by two immutable things, in which it is impossible for God to lie, we might have strong consolation, who have fled for refuge to lay hold of the hope set before us. This hope we have as an anchor of the soul, both sure and steadfast, and which enters the Presence behind the veil, where the forerunner has entered for us, even Jesus, having become High Priest forever according to the order of Melchizedek.

When we are anchored to Jesus, we are anchored to the One who cannot fail, the One who cannot lie, the One who cannot lose. When we throw our hope beyond the veil, faith transforms that hope into an anchor that takes hold of Jesus, our high priest, our provider, our healer, our deliverer. This is powerful!

Be encouraged today. You may have dropped the wrong anchor. You may have failed. You may have messed up. But nothing can separate you from the love of God. Nothing! Something good is coming on the other side of this storm. Power. Provision. Divine appointments. Open doors. All you have to do in the meantime is get anchored right.

Drop Four Anchors

In his book *Six Hours One Friday*, Max Lucado writes about the houseboat he owned in 1979, or, as he put it, "a leaky barge." Hurricane David was making its way toward Florida, sure to sweep devastation over where his boat was docked on the Miami River. Lucado enlisted the help of his friends to secure the vessel. Being inexperienced in boating and novices to hurricanes, together they tied down the leaky barge to dock posts, trees, and even itself. Lucado said his boat looked like it got trapped in a spider web.

A man walked by at the same time these men were tying down the boat. Suntanned and sporting leathery skin, he was something of a sailor. A living legend, more like it. He offered the young men some advice. "Tie her to the land and you'll regret it. Those trees are going to get eaten up by the 'cane. Your only hope is to anchor deep. Place four anchors in four different locations, leave the rope slack, and pray for the best."[3]

Anchor deep. What a profound thought. Your only hope is to anchor deep in God.

Our ultimate anchor must be Jesus. First and foremost. When we start drifting in life, which is a very natural thing to do in and out of a storm, unless we are anchored in Christ, we are going to fall into temptation, into hopelessness, into restlessness, into apathy.

This story reminds me of when the apostle Paul went through a devastating storm on his way to Rome. It was so bad that one of the first things the sailors did was lighten the load of their ship, throwing over the cargo and then the ship's tackle. More than a week later, without food or drink or hope, Paul told them about a message he received from God. They were all going to survive, he said, but they were going to get shipwrecked on an island. By the end of the second week adrift at sea, the sailors sensed they were nearing land. What did they do to avoid running aground on the rocks? They dropped four anchors from the stern and prayed for day to come.[4]

While Jesus should always be at our center, there are other anchors we need to drop that will support us in the storms. I've got four anchors for you that will keep you afloat when times get tough:

- The anchor of purpose
- The anchor of courage
- The anchor of worship
- The anchor of church

Drop the Anchor of Purpose

Two things about purpose: One, your purpose predates your conception (see Jeremiah 1:5). Second, your purpose was planned without your input. God has a reason why He put you on this earth, and He didn't ask your opinion. He put something in you that you might not even realize is there which is unstoppable, as long as you are doing what God has called you and purposed for you to do.

Note that your purpose does not change in a storm. So focus on the purpose. Focus on what is ahead of you, not what you're going through. Jesus was able to make it through His Friday afternoon storm on the cross because of what He saw—His purpose. He knew what would happen on the other side of the crucifixion. He knew Sunday was coming.

Your purpose does not change in a storm.

When Paul was in a dark place in the storm, hanging on to the ship for dear life for weeks as waves crashed around him, God reminded him of his purpose. "Do not be afraid, Paul; you must be brought before Caesar; and indeed God has granted you all those who sail with you."[5] Paul was destined to stand before Caesar in Rome. His purpose was greater than the storm.

Know there is a divine purpose connected to your life. Don't let the storm stop you from fulfilling that purpose.

Drop the Anchor of Courage

Get some courage when the storm comes. We do not give up in the middle of a storm. Nor do we fall to pieces. We stand up tall, knowing Jesus is with us and knowing we can make it with Him through this storm. We may grieve. We may hurt. We may be broken. We may feel devastated. But draw out from your heart a spirit of courage. Remember, if God is for you, who can be against you?

I like to say courage is the ability to finish the race even if you are in last place. Courage is standing up to your teenager when he or she wants to do something you know will be dangerous. Courage is forgiving a friend who let you down. Courage is loving a husband or wife in the midst of a financial crisis that he or she caused. Courage is refusing to let cancer steal your smile. Courage is trying again, dreaming again. Courage is not the absence of fear—it's going through in spite of fear.

Drop the Anchor of Worship

The anchor of worship really speaks to my life because it has been one of the keys that has gotten me through my toughest times. Christians are not supposed to whine in a storm. We are supposed to worship. Many times we worship God for what He has done or what He has allowed us to go through. We must learn how to worship Him for who He is, the captain of the sea.

Worship is God's address. When you begin to worship Him, He shows up. When you feel all hope is lost, throw your hands up, open your mouth with a broken heart and begin to worship God. In worship the answers will come. In worship the victory will come. In worship the breakthrough will come. Worship will keep you grounded wherever God has called you to stay.

Drop the Anchor of Church

When I think about the anchor of church, I think about my childhood. What kept me from becoming a drug addict in my youth? What kept me from sleeping around with girls when I was a teenager? What kept me from living an immoral life? What kept me from becoming an alcoholic? My parents dropped an anchor in our home early on, church. And because we were planted in the house of God, I could only drift so far. The power of the covenant that my parents had made with God for me held me back from many tragic, terrible things. When you get problems, don't run from the Body of Christ. We are not a bunch of perfect people. But we are a people who love God and love others.

If you are newly married and starting a family, drop an anchor in the local church. Start your life together right. Hebrews 10:25 reminds us not to forsake the assembling of ourselves. This is a powerful anchor. No church is perfect. No leadership is perfect. But if you find a place where the pastor preaches the Word of God, get planted in that house. Start connecting with other believers. Start serving. Start giving. There is power in being anchored in the Body of Christ.

Isaiah 65:8 tells us that "the new wine is found in the cluster, and one says, 'Do not destroy it, for a blessing is in it.'" I did not understand this Scripture when I first read it. I mean, technically, the wine is in the bottle, not in the cluster, right? But that is not what God said—the wine *is* in the cluster.

The cluster represents unity and togetherness. The enemy wants to pluck you off the vine. He wants to disconnect you from your relationship with God and with believers who are on the vine. But if you stay in the cluster, the wine will come.

So when you are going through a storm and get discouraged, keep going to your church. Get around Christians. Pray together with fellow believers. The wine is not found when you get plucked away, it's in the cluster. As long as we have unity in the cluster, the wine will flow.

I love what the Scriptures say about this: "Behold, how good and how pleasant it is for brethren to dwell together in unity! It is like the precious oil upon the head, running down on the beard, the beard of Aaron."[6] In other words, where there is unity, there is anointing. Keep the anointing in your home. Keep it in your family. Keep it in your workplace. Keep it in your community. Keep it in your church. Keep it in your leadership team. Keep it in your school. Support one another. Build one another up. Depend on one another. Pray for one another. Let the wine be harvested through your cluster.

Victory Comes Little by Little

When you are in the place God has called you to and it's windy, cold and rainy, know that victory and success through it is yours. It's not up for debate. It's going to happen. And we've got a good idea about how God is going to do this from Deuteronomy:

> You shall not be terrified of them; for the LORD your God, the great and awesome God, is among you. And the LORD your God will drive out those nations before you *little by little*; you will be unable to destroy them at once, lest the beasts of the field become too numerous for you.
>
> Deuteronomy 7:21–22, emphasis added

Victory was the promise here for the nation of Israel. It is the same promise for you today. God will get you through the storm and uncover acres of diamonds. But there is this matter of timing. Notice how it unfolds in this Scripture: *little by little*. It is not instant because God is deliberate about it. Victory will come little by little—and why? *Lest the beasts of the field become too many and devour you.*

The Bible teaches that God will not withhold good things from those who walk uprightly.[7] He will provide everything you need. His very nature is to bless you with victory and success. God wants you to win! He wants to show you how much He loves you so that you will be powerfully favored, supernaturally gifted and abundantly successful. This is good news! But it also requires balance. The progress to your promised land may not be at the rate and at the speed you think it should be.

> *Our greatest blessing is to know Jesus and to be known by Him.*

Uncovering acres of diamonds, especially in the midst of the storm, can seem as though it's taking forever. It's frustrating. *Why is this taking so long? What's the problem?* The issue is not really a *what*; the issue is a *who*. And the answer is God. He is the one who has slowed you down because He loves you for who you are, not what you do.

Your relationship with God should supersede what you do. Too many times we want to be the biggest, the fastest, the smartest, the most successful and the greatest, and in the process we neglect who we are in relationship with Jesus. What we want to do or have happen in our lives should always be overshadowed by who we want to be in Christ.

Our greatest blessing is not our gifting, our talent, our successes or our dreams coming true. Our greatest blessing is to know Jesus and to be known by Him.

Yes, victory and success will come if you follow the Lord. But it will not be instantaneous success. There's unrest. There's toil. There's hardship. There are storms. God allows us to walk through frustration and unease, but He wants us to walk through it with Him. If we anchor correctly, He can teach us how to stay on our knees, how to draw closer and stay close to Him, how to grow our dependence on Him, how to keep Him first and foremost in our lives. And, little by little, we get through to the other side.

If God has you on a slower pace, it is to prepare you for what He's taking you toward, so that when you get there, it will not be about that or about you. It will be about Him.

So stay right where you are. Stay where God has you. And get anchored right to Jesus Christ, the rock of our salvation. As uncomfortable and stormy as it is, He is bringing you into freedom little by little.

❖ 8 ❖

Focus on the Positive

When we cannot see acres of diamonds, it likely means we are in a transition. In this season God is moving us from where we are into where He wants us to be. It's like going from being single and in control of your own life to being a healthy spouse in a healthy marriage; it doesn't happen in an instant. You have to get through the transition period. I have often said that when a couple first gets married, it's ideal. A few months later, when real life sets in, it's an ordeal. A few more months after that, some couples think they got a raw deal. And after more time has passed, some are ready for a new deal.

I am amazed at how many couples get married and a month later question their decision-making ability. They think their new relationship status should not include conflict or require extra effort. They just believe they are going to cakewalk into their destiny of marriage. They have this perfect picture of what it's going to look like, too. The white picket fence. The perfectly manicured lawn. The hardworking, romantic husband. The doting wife with mad cooking skills. The beautiful, sweet children who never mis-behave. Then reality sets in. The grass is knee-high. The house needs a new roof. The children break the white picket fence. The husband spends most of his time at home zoning out. The wife hates cooking and cannot stop nagging. Okay, okay. I know some of these examples are stereotypes, but you get where I'm going. Transitions involve our expectations, most of which are usually unrealistic.

When the unrealistic picture you have in your mind shatters, the enemy will whisper in your ear, "You made a mistake. What are you doing? Why did you get married? You messed up. Time to give up." That is a spirit of negativism right there. When life starts to look a lot less like the fairy tale that you pictured, whether you are in transition or not, it is easy for the enemy to attack and cause you to turn negative.

A Promise and a Negative Report

When the nation of Israel was coming out of the wilderness and was close to crossing over into the Promised Land, they were in a transition. The promise was right in front of them, but a spirit of negativism had overtaken their hope. Seems as though the Israelites never learned their lesson. They hadn't benefited from any of their murmuring or negative talk in the past. And now, on the heels of entering the Promised Land, the negativity was get-ting even louder.

With a set of detailed instructions, Moses dispatched twelve spies to scout out the land of Canaan. These men were tasked with assessing the land and the people who lived there, whether they were weak, strong, few or many. I find it interesting that right in the middle of this set of instructions, Moses told the spies, "Be of good courage."[1] Even before they would face the challenge, he wanted them to be armed with courage. God is saying the same thing to you today. Whatever situation you are going into, whatever mountain looms before you, don't set out with negativism and fear. Be courageous.

When the spies came back, most of them were discouraged. They returned with what Scripture calls an "evil report."[2] Now, Moses had asked them not only to assess the land and its people but to bring back some fruit. The land was so fertile that the cluster of grapes they brought back had to be carried by two men. Can you imagine?

When the spies showed the fruit to Moses, the first thing they told him was actually positive. The land truly flowed with milk and honey. Now watch this—the next thing they said was, "Nevertheless . . ."[3] And the men began to list the bad stuff. "The people who live there are powerful. Some are even giants. We're like grasshoppers compared to them. The city is huge, impenetrable." And so on. The spies had just one good thing to say about the land. That's it. Just one. They knew every detail of the bad information and could only remember one good thing they saw. That's the spirit of negativism at work. Negative people seek to gather information to support their position. They ignore good information and overemphasize bad information.

Out of the ten spies, only two, Joshua and Caleb, refused to feed into that spirit of negativism. While the people of Israel started murmuring after hearing the spies' report, Caleb offered a different perspective. He shook loose from that negative spirit. "Let's take them on!" he roared with confidence. Caleb believed that with God's help every giant that stood in their way could be conquered, even when others said it was impossible. Not everyone shared Caleb's opinion. When the people heard the negative report, you know what they did? They started weeping. In fact, the Bible tells us they cried all night.[4]

It's funny. God never told Moses to tell the spies to check out giants. Nor did He ask them to notice how indefensible the walls of the city were. He never mentioned these things because they were not relevant. When God heard the report from the spies, remember what Scripture called it? An evil report.[5] God didn't call it a factual report. He didn't say it was well thought out, deep or even thorough. Because these men came back with such a negative report, God called it evil. It was so evil to Him, in fact, that He banished every single person age twenty and up, save two, from entering the land of Canaan. I can hear Him say, "I'll let you walk yourself to death before I'll let you go into your Promised Land with that negative, ugly spirit on you."[6] Ouch!

Caleb and Joshua were the only two people exempt from the judgment. God saw in Caleb a "different spirit,"[7] a better spirit—not a spirit of negativism.

Wonder what you're not walking into because of your negative spirit? I can tell you one thing for sure. You cannot walk into your destiny when your spirit is steeped in negativism. Know that you have a choice in the matter. You can feed the spirit of negativism or, like Caleb, take on a different spirit. It is not up to God. It is up to you.

It's Easy to Be Negative

The enemy loves to attack you when you are believing for something God has promised you. You may be trying to start or expand your business. You may be trying to grasp a promise found in Scripture. You may be trying to unify your family. You may be trying to restore your marriage. God's word to you right now is to be filled with courage. Whatever circumstance you find yourself in, you must not deal with it with fear, pessimism and negativity.

I know many people who were raised in negative homes. They were taught to look at life from a negative point of view, to always see the worst-case scenario. If they have a backache, they think, *It's probably cancer*. If they have an ingrown toenail, they tell themselves, *You're going lame. You'll never walk again.*

Our society is saturated with negativism. When is the last time you saw a movie that really uplifted your spirits? When is the last time you watched a television show that didn't have a scene filled with violence, rage or murder? It's about shock value. That seems to be where the money is. I think about how negative the political system has turned. When I watch political elections and campaigns, I often see candidate after candidate slinging mud. It's almost impossible to figure out what these people stand for because their campaigns seem to be all about trashing everyone else. But it works. Why? Because we are a culture that feeds into this negative spirit!

Even the Church can be a feeding machine for the negative. Have you ever met a "cranktified" saint? These kinds of people are plain ol' cantankerous. Sucking their teeth all the time. Rolling their eyes. Some of them can't carry a tune in a bucket, but they waste no time criticizing the worship team and the music.

As believers, we are not supposed to be filled with hopelessness and negativism. No kind of information—that we receive or that we think—has anything to do with the kind of spirit that we have to take on. In order to have victory in our lives, we must keep fighting that spirit of negativism. We must believe what God says and ignore the evil reports.

The enemy knows he cannot stop you from discovering your acres of diamonds unless he attaches a spirit of negativism to you. It is easy to fall into this trap. When you start to get negative, before you know it, you can quickly become wrapped up in a cocoon of negativism. If you begin to feed a negative thought, then another, and another, everything in your life will start to spin out of control. Everything becomes negative. And when you continue to grumble and murmur and complain and find fault, that spirit will attach itself to you and get down deep in your spirit. That is why you have to resist it!

I want to emphasize that I'm not just talking about having a positive attitude instead. This is not about picking yourself up mentally somehow and looking at life in a better way. I am talking about fighting against a real, active spirit of negativism that wants nothing more than to destroy you. If you do not learn how to resist it, it will keep you from reaching what God has planned for you in your Promised Land.

No Right to Be Negative

How many times have you heard someone say (or maybe you have said it yourself), "You just don't understand why I feel the way I feel." Or, "Leave me alone. I have a right to be depressed." Oftentimes, people think they are entitled to be negative, give up or throw in the towel. They will defend their depression. They will defend their dysfunction. They will defend their pity party.

You know what the problem is? None of us have a right to feel that way! Look, people can understand you all the way to the poorhouse. People can sympathize with you all the way to the grave. People who are infected with negativism do not need understanding and sympathy because neither will help. They need correction.

Think about the spies who had returned with the evil report and caused the nation of Israel to cry all night. Think about what

God had done for them up until this point. He had brought them out of Egypt by parting the Red Sea. Miracle! He had swallowed up Pharaoh's whole army so they could not pursue them. Miracle! He had provided them food and water in the wilderness. Miracle after miracle after miracle. The people had no right to be negative.

You have no right to be negative, either. You may not be where you want to be, but think about where you have come from!

Set the Standard

When you have a negative spirit, you just do not want to be happy, and you have a long list of good reasons why you can't be. When a positive person comes around, you are ready to blast away any encouragement or hope they try to give. A negative spirit is always in search of fellowship. Negative people attract negative people. The opposite is true as well.

You have no right to be negative. You may not be where you want to be, but think about where you have come from!

If you remember, Moses handpicked these spies. Each of these men was a leader who represented his entire tribe. Leaders are responsible for making sure a negative spirit does not come on whomever they are leading. In this case, when the spies came back, what happened? With the exception of Joshua and Caleb, they gave a negative report and shoved the nation of Israel tumbling into panic and despair.

If you are a parent, it is your responsibility to make sure the spirit of negativism does not land on your marriage or on your children or in your home. If you are leading in the workplace, your responsibility is to make sure your department, staff or team does not get into a negative funk. If you are in any position of influence, great or small, you are responsible to guard that place from a spirit of negativism. Set the standard. Don't feed into criticism. Don't feed into finding fault. Don't feed into backbiting. Don't feed into complaining. Don't feed into whining.

Watch the kind of people you hang out with. Run away from the gossips. Steer clear of busybodies and faultfinders. Set the standard to keep a spirit of negativism from infecting your situation.

Wait in Expectation

So what is the remedy for the spirit of negativism? Wait in expectation.

When I was a kid, I used to love watching *The Price Is Right*. In this popular TV game show, contestants compete to win cash and prizes by guessing the prices of merchandise. My favorite part was the beginning. In a deep and dramatic voice, the announcer would call out a name from the audience and say, "You're the next contestant on *The Price Is Right!*" The person he called would come down from wherever he or she was sitting and take a place on Contestant's Row. There was more to the show, of course, but I did not care about who would move on to win a refrigerator or a family vacation. I loved the part when the contestant who was called from the audience started freaking out in excitement. He or she would come down the aisle screaming, jumping up and down like crazy, high-fiving everyone around. Funny, these contestants had not even won anything yet. No vacation to Hawaii. No fancy appliance. No sports car. Nothing. They got excited at the mere possibility of winning.

I wish Christians would quit waiting on the victory before expecting to see God's great and mighty power in their midst. We do not have to see it. We do not have to have it. But we should be excited with expectation at the chance of getting a miracle. We should be jumping up and down, expecting God to uncover acres of diamonds in our lives.

In Luke 3, John talks about the baptism of the Holy Spirit and fire.

> Now as the people were in expectation, and all reasoned in their hearts about John, whether he was the Christ or not, John answered, saying to all, "I indeed baptize you with water; but One mightier than I is coming, whose sandal strap I am not worthy to loose. He will baptize you with the Holy Spirit and fire."
>
> Luke 3:15–16

This passage is significant because from the time of Malachi, the last book of the Old Testament, the Jews had waited through four hundred years of silence from God. He refused to speak to the people of Israel. No prophets. No burning bushes. Nothing. Fast-forward four hundred years, and in this passage we get a clue as to the atmosphere the Holy Spirit wanted the people to create so that He could be poured into it.

If God is going to do something, He is going to look for people who have expectation.

The New English Bible translation says the people were not only in expectation, they were "on the tiptoe of expectation." If God is going to do something, He is going to look for people who have expectation. We need to start getting up on our tiptoes and expect God to do the impossible again. This is how we bind the spirit of negativism.

Today, expect God to pour out His Spirit on you, your family, on the people all around you. Expect pain to leave your body. Expect to be healed. Expect to receive a miracle. Expect to be delivered from alcoholism, drug addiction, fear, depression, defeat.

Psalm 119:126 says, "It is time for You to act, O LORD, for they have regarded Your law as void." In other words, when you see people around you disregarding God and His Word, bound by the spirit of negativism, that's not a time to digress. It's not a time to be depressed. It's not a time to lock arms with them. It's a time to get up on tiptoes in expectation.

Expect to Receive

The power of expectation jumps out of Acts 3. Here we learn about a man who was lame since birth. He was brought to the Temple daily to beg for alms. On this particular day, he encountered Peter and John, who had come to the Temple during the prayer hour. I have heard a lot of sermons preached saying that what happened next was dependent upon Peter and John, who saw the man and said, "Silver and gold I do not have, but what I do have I give you: In the name of Jesus Christ of Nazareth, rise up and walk" (verse 6).

Now, I know that power is in the name of Jesus, but notice it did not activate itself. The miracle the lame man received was dependent upon what he did one verse earlier, in Acts 3:5: He looked at Peter and James, "expecting to receive something from them." This man said, "I don't hope. I don't think. I don't believe. I *expect*. I *will* receive something from these men of God." He got even more than what he expected, too. He got a miracle. He got healed!

Expectation is the breeding ground for miracles.

Your greatest miracles are not behind you. So don't look back—look ahead. Understand that something is going to happen that you have not yet seen. God may have done great things for you, but that is not all He's got. "Eye has not seen, nor ear heard, nor have entered into the heart of man the things which God has prepared for those who love Him."[8] You've got to keep going. You've got to get on your tiptoes with a spirit of expectation.

No matter how devastated your field may be, no matter how big the failure, no matter how dark the hallway, no matter how great the pressure, no matter how challenging the transition, you've got to believe that God saves the best for now. That's the power of expectation.

You serve a God that is greater than your faith. You serve a God that is greater than your prayer life. "For God is not unjust to forget your work and labor of love which you have shown toward His name."[9] For God to forget you, He would have to be unrighteous, and that is impossible. It is impossible for God to forget what He has promised you. And so, the only question is, Are you expecting?

I heard a story once about three golfers. Two are excellent. The third is terrible. The bad golfer tees off first. The ball sails through the air. No one can tell where it lands. He is not hopeful.

The other two tee off. Their shots fly off toward the center of the fairway. The three friends hop in a golf cart and speed off toward the green. Only two balls are there, both belonging to the good golfers. The bad golfer starts looking around for his ball. Used to losing a lot of balls, he figures his probably landed in the woods somewhere.

Just before one of the good golfers tries to hit his ball in the hole, he realizes a ball is already in there. The bad golfer reaches down, picks up the ball, looks at it strangely and says, "Can you believe that someone not only left a ball in here, but it's exactly like mine?"

The other two golfers laugh and say, "That is pretty amazing! Imagine that!"

About the same time, a golf pro who works the course pulls up right next to the three friends. "Hey, folks," he says. "Me and some of my co-workers were standing right over there and saw your hole in one. It was pretty incredible. Which one of you made that shot?"

I'm sure by now you know the end of the story. The hole in one belonged to the bad golfer. The incredible thing is that none of them even considered that ball could have been his, not even the bad golfer himself! All three thought it was just a strange coincidence the ball in the hole looked the same as the one he had played with. None of them were even open to the possibility the bad golfer could have made a good shot. In their eyes, it was impossible.

I want you to get to a place where you are not shocked when you look down and see your ball in the cup. I want you to believe in and see the positive in situations, not the negative. I want you to be open to the possibility that your miracle can come, your breakthrough can happen, your battle can be won and your prayer can be answered. I want you to expect to receive!

We need to understand that if God is going to do something, He will look for people who have expectation. So, today, believe for a victory. Believe for a miracle. Whether it has to do with your physical body, a relationship with a loved one, your marriage, your children, your job or a dream, I challenge you to wait on God on the tiptoe of expectation. Expect God to do a work in your life. Expect Him to complete the work He already started. Believe He can restore what has been broken. Break the spirit of negativism by waiting with expectation.

You don't have to see it to believe. Start now. Praise in expectation. Sow in expectation. Pray in expectation. Expect the outpouring of the Holy Spirit in every area of your life. It's tiptoe time for you!

9

Take This Job and Love It

In 1997 Bryan Boyd was enjoying a comfortable stint in corporate America. The 75-year-old owner of a local company called Gunter Construction sought him out and said, "I'd love to sell you my company." Bryan did not have much money, but he saw an opportunity. Owning a fleet of tractors and bulldozers had been his dream since he was in college, and over the years he had trusted God that it would happen.

Bryan and his wife, Susan, made a lot of sacrifices for the business. They moved to a different part of town, into Susan's parents' house. They sold furniture and pinched pennies. It was during this time that the couple got plugged into Free Chapel, planting roots in our church and in the community that would grow deeper over time.

The business grew—and fast. It got to the point where it had grown as much as it could without investing a substantial amount of capital into it. Capital Bryan didn't have. But he was good at what he did, a fact made obvious by the success of his company. Bryan moved so many tractors and bulldozers that he caught the attention of a major company that manufactures agricultural and construction machinery.

An executive from this company noticed how valuable Bryan was for the industry. He was so impressed that he offered him a lucrative package to come work for him. The deal was tempting. It included a ten-year contract with a salary three times what Bryan was currently making. This would provide job stability and secure a comfortable, to say the least, financial position for his family of six. But it came at a price. Bryan would have to uproot and move to another state hundreds of miles away. The job would be demanding and require international travel. Bryan would not be able to have dinner with his family every night. They would also be disconnected from the spiritual community and roots his family had worked hard to build. Bryan and Susan wrestled with this decision for months. They talked about it at length. They prayed. They fasted. Bryan lay awake many nights, rehearsing the pros and cons in his head. Ultimately, he felt that the right thing to do was to stay put. In fact, he felt God speak to him in his heart. *Don't sell the business. I have bigger plans for you.*

Bryan graciously declined the generous offer.

He and his wife made the leap and decided to grow where they were. They made more sacrifices. Over time it paid off. The reputation of his company spread like wildfire and resulted in tremendous growth and a substantial increase in profit. In saying no to the amazing offer, Bryan is providing jobs for thousands of men and women and making more money than if he had said yes. It looked like diamonds on the surface, but it could have been bait to move him away from the acres of diamonds God had for him. Bryan says, "We made a decision based on principle and were rewarded based on that decision."

When God calls us to stay in a certain place, particularly in a workplace, we often do not know why at first. Nor do we know how everything is going to pan out. One thing is certain: There is a purpose in where He has us. Sometimes what looks like a better job or position can pull you away from the acres of diamonds God has for you where you are planted. Bryan could have said yes to something that shined with brilliance on the surface, but he chose to trust God instead and stay where he was.

Bryan and Susan have been a huge blessing, not only to our ministry but to me and my family. Bryan has served as the committee chairman for our main campus in Gainesville. In fact, I remember when we broke ground on the 150 acres we have. I sat in one of the bulldozers from his company and with three-year-old Drake on my lap moved the first bucket of dirt on the property. Bryan also sits on our board of directors and has been very influential in helping us win souls for Jesus around the world. Today, his children are a part of his prospering business, helping continue the legacy of his family.

I wonder what would have happened had Bryan gone for the money in apparently greener pastures. For sure, he would not have had a multigenerational and prosperous business. Nor would he and his family's influence in our church, in the community and around the world have been as huge as it is. It would have all been forfeited for a bigger salary.

Never trade influence with people for money. The Bible tells us, "Choose a good reputation over great riches; being held in high esteem is better than silver or gold" (Proverbs 22:1 NLT). Whenever I make a decision, I keep this in mind. I can always make money, but I do not ever want to lose people.

I don't know if you love your job or if you hate it, but I want you to know you are where you are for a reason. Your workplace is your place of influence. Even if you cannot see it, it is a field strewn with diamonds. This truth may be hard to realize if you feel stuck in a job in which you feel underpaid, undervalued and unnoticed. If this describes you, I want to encourage you. Do not minimize the influence you have over your employees, your co-workers and your team.

Let me put it this way. You have influence with the people you work with that I, as a preacher, will never have. There is no hope of me winning the world for Jesus. It is only going to happen when every Christ follower uses his or her influence wherever he or she is planted to make an impact in and for His name.

Work Is Worship

In the Jewish way of thinking, work and worship are connected. You can see this in the Hebrew word *avodah*, which means "work, worship and service." You can even say that work is worship. You may not view the accountant crunching numbers in an office as an act of worship, but if she is doing it in the name of Jesus, God does.

Did you know that of all of Jesus' parables, 80 percent of them had a workplace context? Did you know that of all of Jesus' public appearances recorded in the Bible, nearly all occurred in the marketplace? What does this tell us? Work is a part of everyday life. Work matters!

Now think about this. Jesus was not born into a super religious family in the community, like that of a priest. God chose to send His Son into the home of a carpenter. A middle-class, blue-collar home. I imagine dinnertime conversation in Jesus' home did not revolve around religious law debates. I'm sure Joseph rattled off work talk. "Did we get that order of wood, Jesus?" "Are we almost finished making the table for the family down the road?" "I think we need another few weeks to finish that barn."

Jesus would stay in the workforce with his father for at least twenty years before He would ever be released for the last three and a half years of his life into His ministry. The Son of God spent more time in the workforce than in ministry. Jesus was as much in the will and purpose of God when He was sawing wood, making tables and constructing chairs as He was when He was teaching, healing the sick and raising the dead.

Another thing I find interesting is that before Jesus was crucified, He carried His cross through the marketplace. The Via Dolorosa wasn't a back road through the middle of nowhere. It was a street that wound through the busy marketplace. We've got enough crosses in the Church. We need some crosses in the workplace. We need people who will shine their light for God and exemplify the life of Jesus in retail stores, startups, corporations and home businesses.

Keep in mind, you were not hired to be an evangelist on the job. You were hired to perform a specific task. Sometimes where we are in the workplace seems unsatisfying. Sometimes we have unrealistic expectations of needing to bond with our bosses or needing the leadership team to care about our families or our financial situations. Whether we love our jobs or don't, we must focus on doing our jobs and doing them with excellence. If work is worship, you must do it with all your heart. You must perform well.

Affect Your Environment by Standing Out

When God put Adam in the Garden to cultivate it,[1] He was in essence telling Adam to affect the culture of his workplace. This is God's commandment to every one of you today.

I love this verse in Isaiah:

Arise, shine; for your light has come! And the glory of the LORD is risen upon you. For behold, the darkness shall cover the earth, and deep darkness the people; but the Lord will arise over you, and His glory will be seen upon you. The Gentiles shall come to your light, and kings to the brightness of your rising. Lift up your eyes all around, and see: They all gather together, they come to you; your sons shall come from afar, and your daughters shall be nursed at your side.

Isaiah 60:1–4

In this passage, *Gentiles* refers to those who do not know God. Think about the people you work with who are spiritually lost. Think about this place of influence God has given you. "Arise and shine"—in other words, stand up and stand out. God does not want His people in a dark world hiding the light He has given them.

You are His acres of diamonds to the lost. If you are going to attract the attention of those in your workplace for Jesus, stand up and stand out. If you are in business, do it right. If you work in education, do it right. If you work in the sports field, do it right. Whether you sell T-shirts or support an executive, do it right. This is a biblical principle.

So, what are some ways you can stand out and uncover or shine as acres of diamonds where you work?

- Get anointed.
- Have an excellent spirit.
- Develop an "and then some" attitude.

Get Anointed

Anointing is anointing. There is no greater anointing for someone in the ministry than there is for someone who works a secular job or stays home and cares for the family. The anointing on a preacher is the same anointing on you. If God reserved His power only for a church environment, He would limit His possibilities. God can perform His work anywhere: in church, at home, at work, in the grocery store!

What is the anointing? It's not a scary or super-spiritual term that should weird you out. Simply put, it's the Holy Spirit activated in your life. I do not dare walk onto a platform Sunday morning without preparing my soul for my calling. I read my Bible. I pray. I meditate. I seek God. I ask Him to lead, guide and give me wisdom. I take my anointing seriously. You should, too.

Whether you love your job or hate it, God can use you where you are. So before you clock in, take time to pray. Approach the start of your day by seeking God and asking the Holy Spirit to activate Himself in your life. Ask Him to show you opportunities to serve or to be a blessing to others. God has called you to your place of influence for a reason.

When you are empowered with the anointing, it enhances what you are gifted to do. You may not be working your dream job right now or using all your talents where you are, but you are where you are because you can do something. You may be gifted to sell, create or draw. You may have a knack for numbers, gadgets or technology. You may have a talent for music, an eye for detail or incredible organization skills. If you let it, the anointing can come on your life to enhance what you are already gifted to do.

Before the battle with Goliath, David was already gifted to fight. He had killed a bear. He had killed a lion. And when the anointing came on him, he killed Goliath. Nothing is more powerful than an anointed professional on the job. Whatever you do for a living, God wants to anoint you to be successful. God wants to anoint you to carry the cross in the marketplace.

The workforce is going to change for the better when you use your power and influence for Jesus. Not because you're preaching all the time to every person who crosses your path. Not because you pray in tongues out loud over your lunch. Not because you leave your ten-pound large-print Bible on your desk. You will affect the culture of your workplace when you do your job, when you do it well and when you stand out for Jesus through your behavior and your actions. And, believe me, you need the anointing to do this!

You need the wisdom of the Holy Spirit to make the right business call, to hire the right person, to know if and when to close a deal. You need the fruits of the Spirit to encourage your co-workers instead of tear them down, to effect a positive instead of a negative attitude and to get along with difficult people.

As you prepare for work tomorrow, spend time with God before you start your day. This does not have to mean praying for two hours in deep intercession. Just create a quiet space before the rest of the house wakes up. Unplug from your phone and social media. Take a breath and acknowledge the presence of and your need for the Lord. Ask Him to give you His anointing over all that you do. Ask Him to enhance the talents, skills and gifts He has given you that help accomplish your assignments. Ask Him for wisdom in how you manage your time and your responsibilities and how you interact with the people around you.

Have an Excellent Spirit

In the Bible, we read that Daniel "distinguished himself above the governors and satraps, because an excellent spirit was in him; and the king gave thought to setting him over the whole realm."[2] Daniel had an excellent spirit. This is what set him apart for great success. We need to ask God to help develop in us an excellent spirit.

What does this mean? It means two things. One, whatever you do, you do it well. Two, you have a good attitude while doing it. When we have an excellent spirit, we exemplify Jesus.

Daniel was impeccable in his willingness to be great for God, even in the terrible environment in which he lived. When he was young he, along with many other young men who were the smartest and most gifted in the Hebrew nation, was taken into captivity by King Nebuchadnezzar of Babylon. The king used these gifted men to build his kingdom. He changed everything about them. For three years, these young men, including Daniel, were put through an intense conversion process in which they were stripped of their Hebrew heritage and identity and taught the language and culture of the Babylonians. As much power as he exerted over these men, the king knew he could not really change them until he changed their worship. He knew as long as they worshiped their God in his culture, they would always be connected to God.

So King Nebuchadnezzar forced these Jewish men to bow down before him. While everyone in the kingdom obeyed, Daniel refused. This young man made a decision in his hostile environment to serve God, not man. Each time Daniel chose God over the king, he put himself at great personal risk and was reprimanded harshly. And in each instance, God miraculously saved him. Ultimately, Daniel was promoted to a leadership role. He served as the chief advisor to the king and later as top ruler of the entire kingdom.

You might recall that early on, Daniel refused to eat the choice food served in the palace. He asked one of King Nebuchadnezzar's high officials to allow him and the other Hebrew men to eat according to the Law of God for ten days and prove that their diet was superior to the king's nutritional plan. Daniel set a standard.

When the time was up, Daniel and the other men looked better, felt better and were sharper mentally and physically. Daniel took a stand to prove that he could do more with God than even with the king. This high standard elevated him to a position in which he had power over the heathen nation of Babylon.

Daniel had a unique spiritual gift, the ability to interpret dreams. But the thing that impressed the leadership around him more than anything wasn't that. It was the way that he performed. It was the way that he carried himself. Daniel caught the eye of the king because he distinguished himself with an excellent spirit. Daniel was detailed. He was dependable. He was diligent. He had a great attitude. If you gave this young man a vacuum and told him to clean a room, he would do it beyond expectations. He would use all the accessories and vacuum between and under the cushions of the couch, remove the cobwebs in every corner, and even dust the molding around the perimeter of the room. He wouldn't just do a "get by" job. He'd do a "get over" job. This is what it means to have an excellent spirit.

Your performance determines your platform. How you do what you do will determine the influence you have among those around you. People are watching. Not just higher-ups, but everyone. You set the example in how you care for patients, teach students, sell beauty products or flip burgers. When we perform our jobs with excellence, we bring glory and honor to Jesus Christ.

Every part of your life ought to be excellent. Comb your hair. Press your pants. Clean up your desk. Take the trash out of your car. Start getting to work on time. Stop badmouthing the boss. Start getting excited when Monday arrives instead of groaning about it. Being excellent will set you up for success. You will become an asset. You will begin to contribute something positive to your environment. You will shine bright in a dark world.

When I was growing up in our church, our worship team did the best they could, I guess. But I will never forget how it seemed some people put zero effort into it. One guy would never show up to practice. He believed he could just rely on the anointing. He would walk right up on stage right before church, tune up, then start playing. One thing was certain: This guy needed more than just the anointing. Another musician would frequently show up late. One of the singers had a bad habit of forgetting the order of worship. I never believed in just showing up and hoping for the best. Excellence means practice. It means putting your best foot forward. It means preparation. It means committing to a job well done.

Having an excellent spirit has an effect on your character. It hits your integrity. The men whom Daniel ruled over were threatened by his success. They sought to trap him in some impropriety, but as hard as they looked, they could not find any fault in him. They couldn't catch him stealing. They couldn't catch him lying. They couldn't catch him cheating. They couldn't attack Daniel's character because he had an excellent spirit. When you live with excellence, it shows. May we be like Daniel on and off the job. May no one find any corruption in us that would damage our reputation.

When you have an excellent spirit, you can have influence where you work. This makes me think of David. Before he was a king and a giant slayer, David was an excellent musician. He played his harp skillfully. You don't get good at something overnight. He must have practiced for hours on end. Because he played skillfully, he stood out. David began to shine in the kingdom of Israel. That excellence was a natural thing that God used to get spiritual power into that kingdom.

Excellence doesn't start at the top. It doesn't begin when you get big things. It starts when you have a little and you use it well.

If you will not clean up a tiny cubicle with excellence, you will not run a company with it. The Bible gives great advice: Don't despise small beginnings.[3] Being faithful with the small things reaps great rewards. Many people are waiting for a big moment to happen, like a big break. I'll let you in on a secret: Big moments don't come to people who wait for big moments. Big moments are birthed out of being faithful in the seemingly insignificant moments of the routine, the menial, the non-glamorous and unexciting. I like to say it this way: Big doors swing on little hinges.

Big doors swing on little hinges.

If you will become excellent, you will stand out of the crowd. You will earn recognition. When you build a name for yourself, you build your reputation. And people begin to notice. People of authority will want you close to them. They will pull you in. They will start asking your opinion.

Arise and shine. Stand up and stand out. Be excellent in all you do. Be excellent in your attitude. When you do, your light will shine. Remember, the people you work with may not care what church you go to or who your pastor is, but they see what you do and how you do it. They might never read the Bible, but they are reading you.

Develop an "And Then Some" Attitude

It seems the current workplace philosophy in the United States is wanting maximum reward for minimum effort. Many people want to see just how little they can do to get by without getting fired.

I remember taking my oldest daughter, Courteney, on a date one time. We had dinner and planned on seeing a movie afterward. After we got our tickets and secured our seats in the theater, I headed to the lobby to get us some popcorn, candy and drinks. I groaned when I saw the line. It seemed a mile long, snaking around five or six rows of roped-off lanes. A few minutes passed. The line barely moved. Another few minutes passed. Still no movement, and the line was even longer. I noticed there were only three people on the registers behind the counters and a fourth employee, a manager, off to the side. This young lady just stood there watching. From my vantage point it seemed she did not want to jump in to help get the line moving so we could enjoy our movie. Clearly, this employee did not know the "and then some" philosophy.

The difference between a successful person and an average person is three words: *and then some.* If you want to uncover acres of diamonds in your workplace, don't just do what is expected or required. Go the extra mile. Live a lifestyle where you do "and then some." Amazing things will begin to happen.

When God is looking to raise someone up or promote somebody, He looks for people whose performance isn't mediocre. He looks for people who understand the power of doing something extra.

One of my favorite stories in the Bible is about Abraham finding a wife for his son Isaac. In those days, it was a parent's duty to choose the mate for one's child. So Abraham sent his trusted servant, Eliezer, to search for a bride for his son. Abraham's family was one of the wealthiest on the earth. Isaac, handsome and successful, was a most eligible bachelor. He was quite the catch.

So Eliezer took ten camels and loaded them with silver, gold, diamonds and rubies, goods from Abraham's fortune. When he got to the city of Nahor, he stopped by a well in the evening, the time of day when women went out to draw water. What was

Eliezer's criteria for finding a wife for Isaac? It's interesting. The first thing he did was pray.

> O LORD God of my master Abraham, please give me success this day, and show kindness to my master Abraham. Behold, here I stand by the well of water, and the daughters of the men of the city are coming out to draw water. Now let it be that the young woman to whom I say, "Please let down your pitcher that I may drink," and she says, "Drink, and I will also give your camels a drink"—let her be the one You have appointed for Your servant Isaac. And by this I will know that You have shown kindness to my master.
>
> Genesis 24:12–14

Such powerful words! He was looking for a particular attitude in a potential wife for Isaac.

At the same time he was praying, a woman named Rebekah walked up, gracefully balancing a water jug on her shoulder. Eliezer began to watch her as she took the jug and dipped it into the water. He asked her for a drink, and she was more than happy to oblige.

As Eliezer sipped the cool water, she said, almost matter-of-factly, "Sir, by the way, I'd love to give some water to your camels, also."

Hospitality in those days was almost like a law. It was part of the Hebrew custom to treat guests in your home, even strangers, kindly. You would offer them food or water, whatever would bring them refreshment. When Rebekah drew water for Eliezer, she was doing what she was supposed to do, being hospitable. But when she added, "I will water your camels, also," everything changed.

Think about what she was offering. She had ten camels to water. One camel can drink more than forty gallons of water in just a few minutes. That's four hundred gallons of water she had to get from the well. Talk about inconvenient. And so much work! I imagine she just had her nails done. Gotten a facial. Put on pretty clothes. Pulling four hundred gallons of water was going to make her sweat. It was going to make her tired. It was going to make her mascara run and her hair ragged. I imagine most women would have never made the offer. They would have said, "Take care of your own mangy camels, stranger. That is not part of my job description." But there was something about this woman. And because of her work ethic, because she had an over-and-above attitude, Rebekah became the great-great-great (many times over) grandmother of Jesus Christ. She didn't just give; she gave and then some.

If you are on the job and not putting forth an "and then some" effort, you are not shining your light for Jesus, and He will not be able to uncover acres of diamonds where you are. If you want to be an example to your co-workers, your team or your boss, give extra. Do more than what is required. Go over and beyond your job description. If you are a mechanic, don't just fix the car. Wash it for your customer as well. If you are a bank teller, don't just manage transactions. Do it with a smile. Say something encouraging to the man or woman making the deposit. When you do this, you increase your value.

When Rebekah took the three or four or more hours out of her day to water those nasty, mangy camels, she had no idea that those dirty animals were loaded with diamonds, earrings and other precious things. Do not miss this revelation. *There was beauty and wealth—acres of diamonds—under the seemingly insignificant act of an ordinary day and in the ugliness of sweaty camels covered in dirt and dust.* Rebekah's unexpected reward was hidden in going beyond what was required.

Most of us shoot our camels. I don't mean to offend animal lovers when I say this. But we shun the messy places, the dirty places, the ordinary places. In Rebekah's case, the mangy, ugly situation actually became the gateway to a phenomenal future when she watered it instead of cursing it. When she said, "I'll do this and more," instead of, "Ain't my job," she changed her life and her future.

Here's a big idea. The power of doing more than expected pleases God. It makes Him happy. When you do "and then some" on the job when nobody is looking, God notices. He sees what is going on. So do what is right. Go above what is required. God sees the work you do. You may not see purpose in your job. You may be bored out of your mind. You may work in a hostile environment. You are where you are for a reason. And until God releases you from that situation, do it right and do it well. Allow the Holy Spirit to open doors of opportunities and conversations at your workplace that will honor Him.

"And whatever you do, do it heartily, as to the Lord and not to men, knowing that from the Lord you will receive the reward of the inheritance; for you serve the Lord Christ" (Colossians 3:23–24). You are where you are for a great purpose, for such a time as this. There is potential in your present job. Give all you've got! You will dig up hidden treasures there that someone else has not noticed.

❖ 10 ❖

How to Be a Hero

At the time of this book's publication, Cherise and I have been married for more than 32 years. We've gone through plenty of storms in that time. We've learned that unless we hold fast to what God says, our feelings will take over. It has been easy to feel unworthy to serve God because of arguments we've had. It's easy to think we would be better off on our own. It's easy to think that God didn't put us together.

These are all lies the enemy whispers to many of us. When we start to believe the lies, bailing on the marriage seems an obvious choice. But when we run away or leave for someone else, we don't give ourselves a chance to see the acres of diamonds that lie in the fields of our marriages.

In our first year of marriage, Cherise and I had some major challenges. This is probably true of most marriages. My mother-in-law, Pat, and her husband, Jimmy, were instrumental in mentoring us during this time. Just when Cherise and I felt that we couldn't stand each other or take it anymore, Pat and Jimmy would have a sit-down with us, separately. Pat would turn to Cherise and say, "God put you and Jentezen together. You're not coming over to my house. You're going to go back to your house and make things right." Jimmy would take me in another room and say the same to me.

Marriage is brutal on selfishness. A man once told me that after his first few years of marriage, his wife told him, "Cinderella lied. You're neither a prince nor charming." Then she threw a glass slipper at him. In my case, I really believed that in our first year of marriage pretty much every argument Cherise and I got into was her fault. It's true! In my mind, I was practically perfect. I thought if I could make her more like me, we would have the ideal marriage. I was wrong, obviously.

It is easy to lose hope in a marriage when you don't brace that relationship in the Word of God. But when you get your mind right, when you take your thoughts captive, when you stand against the lies of the enemy, God's Word will build you up. I learned how important it was to quote Scripture in these times, verses like Hebrews 13:4, "Marriage is honorable"—or as some translations say, "precious." And Proverbs 5:18, "Rejoice with the wife of your youth." And 1 Corinthians 13, which gives us the best definition of love. Marriage may not feel precious all the time, and you may not feel like rejoicing with your spouse, but build yourself, and your marriage, on these truths. This is seed that will reap acres of diamonds of love, unity and joy in your relationship.

We are, today, in a generation in which happy homes, great marriages and strong families have become endangered species. The home and the family are under the greatest attack. The divorce rates for Christians and non-Christians are the same. If you are divorced, my heart goes out to you. I love you, I accept you and I believe in God's restoration for your life. I also want to say that we must take a strong stand against initiating divorce in our marriages just because things aren't working out, or it's too hard, or we've changed too much, or we've grown apart.

The sovereign vow we made to God on the wedding day is serious business. It is a spiritual covenant we cannot take lightly. I want to encourage you in your marriage. If you are on the brink of divorce because you believe you can get someone better somewhere else, if you are tempted to stray because the fire went out in your marriage, if financial pressure is bearing down on you and you think it's better to call it quits, stay. Stay in that place.

Marriage and family might be the two greatest areas where it is difficult, if not sometimes outright impossible, to see acres of diamonds. But underneath the field of bickering, financial trouble, social pressures, rebellious kids, temptation, mounting responsibilities and much more, God wants to uncover the diamonds of unity, of faith, of victory, of healing, of love—and not just for you, your spouse and your kids, but also for generations to come.

As for Me and My House

Too many times we have an unrealistic picture of what our marriages and families ought to be like. We're going to get married, get involved in church, start having babies, dress them up in cute clothes and take them to church every Sunday in our clean car while singing worship songs the whole way. Definitely unrealistic!

Most times—especially, it seems, on Sunday—all hell breaks loose. This one refuses to go to church. That one forgot how to get dressed. Another one complains the entire time. Your spouse seems to be no help, and the load and pressure of getting everyone out of the house in one piece is crashing down on you.

Cherise and I have five kids. Getting them ready for church when they were young was no easy task. I had it easy—I had to leave before everyone else. A part of me felt relieved needing to be at church early to prepare for the service while my wife was at home trying to wrangle five little ones out the door on time. One Sunday, frustrated out of her mind, Cherise pulled up to church, hustled the kids in the door, made sure someone on staff got them where they needed to go and hightailed it out of the parking lot, a cloud of dust swirling behind. I can't blame her. It's hard!

If you have children, I know what a challenge it is to raise them—and to do it right. It can be difficult to see their potential when they're mouthy, disrespectful and outright rebellious. You may get aggravated because of all the sacrifices you made for your child who is constantly breaking the rules, but God calls you to be a hero and keep praying for them, keep loving them and keep raising them right. You may not see them full of potential, but God does.

I am going to equip you with foundational truths that will strengthen you and your family as you stay in that place.

Start Digging Wells

I talked earlier about how Abraham had built wells for himself and his family. The Middle Eastern climate is hot and dry. Digging wells was hard, putting it mildly. There were no drills or machines around to make the process more efficient. It required blood, sweat, tears and a lot of time. When Abraham dug those wells, he understood that the time and the energy he invested in digging were not just for him and his wife. They were for his son and for generations to follow. This reminds me of the Scripture "A good man leaves an inheritance to his children's children" (Proverbs 13:22). This doesn't just mean money or the house; this is a spiritual inheritance that is eternal.

When Abraham died, the Philistines filled the wells with dirt. The water still flowed under the surface, but there was no way for it to come out. The enemy thought they could drive the next generation out without this source of water. But Isaac, Abraham's son, was willing to fight for the well. Some wells are worth fighting over. If you are in a low place today, if your marriage is on the rocks, if your children are not living for God, if strife and contention are consuming the atmosphere of your home, know this: You are closer to the water than ever before.

Some wells are worth fighting over. . . . You are closer to the water than ever before.

There may have been wells in your life or generations past that flowed with water, with life, with faith, with the power of the Holy Spirit. But maybe the enemy has clogged them up. Maybe today you are reaping the consequences of stopped-up wells. Be encouraged, for you have the same spiritual tools Isaac had to dig them back up. If you dig and keep digging, you are going to hit water. You are going to uncover acres of diamonds of revival in your family.

I want to show you four wells you need to dig to find God's best for you, for your family and for generations to come:

- The well of sacrifice
- The well of discipline
- The well of quality time
- The well of faithfulness

The Well of Sacrifice

Sacrifice has been sacrificed in this generation. We want everything to come easy. You want you and your family to be blessed?

It requires sacrifice. You want an anointing a thousand times stronger than you have ever had? You have to pray. Study the Word. Speak life over your situation. Fast. Believe. Keep believing.

God is not your garbage collector. God is not your Goodwill; you do not give Him your leftovers, the things you don't really want anyway. Faith is not a cruise ship that is all about fun and relaxation. Faith is a battleship. It is time to declare war. Get off social media and get on your knees. Turn off the TV and dial into the Holy Spirit. Stop sleeping in on Sundays and start getting planted in the house of God.

Hebrews 11 is often called the Faith Hall of Fame. This biblical *Who's Who* lists people like Abraham, Jacob, Joseph, Gideon and David, distinguished people in the Kingdom of God who achieved astonishing results through their faith. They subdued kingdoms, quenched the violence of fire, and were valiant in battle (see verses 33–34). Talk about impressive.

Sandwiched in the middle of this roll call, the writer mentions a few people who didn't do anything that on the surface seems powerful or mighty. And yet, God inducted them into this Faith Hall of Fame. These three people were heroes not for their military strategy or their ability to lead nations. They were heroes because they saved their families. They were committed to their loved ones. They sacrificed greatly for them in the name of God. When we make sacrifices to point our family in the direction of the One who gave His life for us, we dig a deep well that will quench their thirst for years to come. We uncover acres of diamonds of spiritual blessings.

Rahab was one of these people. "By faith the harlot Rahab did not perish with those who did not believe, when she had received the spies with peace" (verse 31). When the two spies of Israel were being hunted and hid in Rahab's house, she made a deal with them. "I'll help you if you guarantee my safety and the safety of my parents, siblings and all their families. So when you invade this city and judgment comes on this place, if I can get my family in this house, promise me they will be saved."[1] The spies agreed.

Rahab got her family in the house. This was no easy task. She was a prostitute. It was social suicide for people to be in her house. But she knew if her family was in the house and if she did her part, God would do His part and they would all be saved. Rahab was a hero of faith because she knew the power of being "in the house," which is another way of saying, "in the church."

Want to be a hero in your family? Keep your family in the house of God. Don't ask your teenagers, who have not yet earned the right to have an opinion, whether or not they want to go to church. You get your kids up. You take your family to church. You make the sacrifice. Sometimes the bed is so comfy that it's tempting to stay there, but the only way you are going to reap acres of diamonds in your family is to get them planted in the house.

Noah was another hero in his family. "It was by faith that Noah built a large boat to save his family from the flood" (Hebrews 11:7 NLT). Noah built the ark—a type of church today—not on his own but by involving his entire family in the work of God. For a hundred years, Noah and his sons spent most of their days measuring, cutting, hammering and building. Boat building was the culture of their family. In other words, they worked in the church. They did not just show up on Sunday, sit through the service and leave. They served. They gave. They got connected with others. They dug a well of sacrifice.

Noah was a hero of faith because he got all his children building for the Kingdom. I share some of his joy, because I am immensely proud of my kids today. All of them are working for the Lord and serving in some capacity. Now, they weren't always excited to be a part of what we do. There were times Cherise and I would practically have to drag them to church. They would sit in the service with arms crossed, looking bored and annoyed out of their minds. But my wife and I refused to build our ministry without the kids being involved. They may not have enjoyed every minute of spending a few nights a week in church, but it has paid off. Proverbs 22:6 teaches, "Train up a child in the way he should go, and when he is old he will not depart from it." Your child may seem to have departed from the way of the Lord today, but I want to encourage you to serve God, keep praying and keep believing. God will uncover acres of diamonds in your children in time.

Finally, we have Moses' parents. "By faith Moses, when he was born, was hidden three months by his parents, because they saw he was a beautiful child; and they were not afraid of the king's command" (Hebrews 11:23). This mom and dad were heroes in the eyes of God because they hid their son Moses from the evils of external influences. They protected Moses as long as they could. You are a hero if you learn to hide your children from harmful and destructive external influences. I know one day they will be exposed to the internet, violence, pornography, drinking, drugs and sexual temptations, but as long as you can, protect them from these things. Know what they're doing and where they're going. Know who their friends are. Know what they're listening to and watching. As long as they live in your house, shield them from the filth of this world. When you protect your children in this manner, you set them up for having a life of faith. Diamonds!

Stand firm. Be a hero in your family. Remember, your heavenly Father has already won the war over your family. Don't quit. Keep digging the well of sacrifice. I promise, it will be worth it!

The Well of Discipline

Human beings are sinful. Children are sinful, too. It's natural for kids to be disobedient. It's natural for them to be disrespectful, to talk back. The only thing that will stop a child from spiraling downward is a parent's belief in and enforcement of discipline in the home.

Every parent has his or her own parenting philosophy. And every family dynamic is unique. Some children live in single-parent homes. Some spend certain days or weeks with one parent, then switch off. Some are growing up in blended families. Whatever your situation and style for raising kids, discipline is essential. What you do when they are young sets the stage for when they grow up. Train them to be obedient. Train them to listen. Train them to solve problems on their own. Train them to serve others. Train them to be kind and encouraging. Train them to be respectful.

Re-dig the well of discipline in your home. Your kids may be older, and maybe you fell short in this area when they were younger. You may not be able to make up for lost time, but you can start today to set the right example and teach them the right ways.

The Well of Quality Time

In order for discipline to be effective, you must nurture your relationship with your family. Spend time with them. Families need to have fun together. Take vacations. Go on day trips. Take a ride to the local ice cream shop once a week. Attend a concert together. Have movie or game nights at home. I know, maybe this sounds idyllic. But if you are a parent, you know how overwhelming life can be at home. Sometimes it's good to ditch the norm and take a break together with your family. Let them see your fun side. Let them see you being human. Sometimes when you try to do this, it turns into an epic fail. But at least you'll be able to laugh about it. Sometimes that's just about all you can do. But, hey, laughing is good.

I remember years ago, when the kids were little, we had to get up at six in the morning to take our oldest child, Courteney, to a soccer tournament. She played. We watched. Driving back, every one of our five kids bickered and whined the entire way.

"She touched me!"

"He took my toy!"

"No, it's mine!"

"I'm hungry!"

"Stop looking at me!"

That evening we went to a birthday party at Chuck E. Cheese. Same thing happened on that car ride. Whining. Fighting over the dumbest things. Cherise and I drew a lot of imaginary lines on the way there. Over and over we said, "If you do that one more time, we're going to . . ." Now, this chaos wasn't necessarily out of the ordinary, but I had gotten up way early that morning, and I was tired. It was all beginning to get on my nerves.

The party at Chuck E. Cheese was packed. Loud. Two-plus hours of watching hundreds of crazy little people screaming and running around like rabbits. Toward the end, Connar and Drake, our two youngest children, were in the early stages of a meltdown. We left not long after to avoid a major meltdown. I wanted to go home—and straight to bed.

On the ride home, part three of whining and fighting kicked off. This time the kids bickered over the dinky prizes they had won at the party. Then, out of nowhere, someone suggested ice cream. The kids just had to have it. I said okay. A few minutes later, every child was buckled in and armed with a mouth-watering ice cream cone. We were finally headed home. I'll never forget being stopped at an unusually long red light. I glanced into the rear view mirror and noticed Drake holding a cone. Just a cone. There was no ice cream on the cone. It was all over his face, his shirt, his lap, the seat and the side of the car. He didn't seem to care, but I did. We didn't have any napkins or anything that could clean up the mess. Still stopped at that red light, I started yelling. Cherise started yelling. Then Drake joined in. I rolled down his window and yelled, "Just throw it out, Drake. Just throw out the cone."

When Drake flung that cone out the window, the driver of the car behind me started beeping and yelling out his window, "Litterbug! Litterbug! Pick it up, litterbug!" He didn't do it one time, either. He did it again and again! I'm not proud of this, but I snapped. I yelled at him through the open window. Not one of my proudest moments.

When I pulled my head back in the car, I was shocked by what I heard. Nothing! Deafening silence! No crying. No whining. All the little people in that car sat up straight in their seats like obedient soldiers, eyes wide, mouths shut.

Then, a little person's voice piped up from the backseat. "Oooh, Daddy," Caroline scolded, "you're in trouble. I'm going to tell Maggie House!" Maggie was one of her friends in church. The two of them had a knack for spreading news like wildfire. I didn't say anything. No one else did, either. Then, almost in unison, we all busted out laughing. Cherise and I laughed so hard tears rolled down our faces.

Laugh with your kids. Be there for them. Show up to the soccer game. Show up to the play. Show up to the dance recital. Take your child out on date nights once a month. Read with them before they go to bed. Get out and have fun with your family. There's nothing like it!

The Well of Faithfulness

A faithful man will abound with blessings.[2] Paul taught that "it is required in stewards that one be found faithful" (1 Corinthians 4:2). You are responsible for stewarding your family. Are you faithful in your marriage? Are you faithful in providing for your family? Are you faithful in doing the right things? Are you faithful in God's house? Are you faithful in creating an environment of faith in your home? When you are faithful, you will ultimately see acres of diamonds from the fruit of your sacrifice.

My parents dug a well of faithfulness, and I could not get away from it! I was blessed to have a mom and dad who loved God and their family. They led us in the faith as a lifestyle. In church and at home, my parents were faithful. I am incredibly glad for the influence they had on my life, because it was a huge blessing!

I know not everyone had exemplary parents growing up, but if you have children, you can be one for them. Dig the well of faithfulness. One of the most influential ways to do this is through praying regularly. You pray them through that twelve-year-old rebellious stage. You pray them through thirteen, when hormones are raging and they are noticing, big time, the opposite sex. You pray them through fifteen, you pray them through sixteen, you pray them through eighteen and going off to college. You pray them through their entire lives!

Your Children Are God's Weapons

When you dedicate your children to the Lord, you put them in a spiritual safehouse. Sometimes we need God to help us open our eyes to see the potential in our children. You may see your kid as sweet or shy, impulsive or studious, rebellious or obedient, but God sees them in a completely different light. He sees them as weapons.

> Behold, children are a heritage from the LORD, the fruit of the womb is a reward. Like arrows in the hand of a warrior, so are the children of one's youth. Happy is the man who has his quiver full of them; they shall not be ashamed, but shall speak with their enemies in the gate.
>
> Psalm 127:3–5

When God saved you, He did not just think of *you* being saved. He also saw in you another generation, and another generation, and another generation that He would save. It's never just about you. When God looks at us, He sees multigenerational beings. The acres of diamonds of spiritual blessing can extend far beyond our own lives on earth.

God does not see our children as just flesh and blood. God does not see our children as just cute. God does not see our children as just a gift that He gives us. God does not give us children just so we can experience the emotions of parenthood. When God gives a righteous couple children, it is because He sees those children as weapons. He sees them as arrows of deliverance. He sees them as arrows making a difference in His name. He sees them as arrows piercing the darkness.

Sometimes we as parents need to be reminded of the big picture. We are not put on this earth just to have a good time or so that we can raise children who wear cool clothes, win high school basketball tournaments, or go to Ivy League universities. We are bows that send the arrows of our children out into the world for God to use for His purposes.

So whether you are starting to plan your family, whether you have teenage children or whether you find yourself in a blended family, think about how you are projecting your children into this world. Are you sending them off in the right direction? Are you sending them toward partying or fighting or bitterness or addiction? In what direction are you, the bow, projecting the spiritual arrows of the children God has entrusted to you?

He sees those children as weapons. He sees them as arrows of deliverance. He sees them as arrows making a difference in His name. He sees them as arrows piercing the darkness.

Sadly, I believe a lot of arrows are broken in the quiver. Before they can even get out, our children are torn by negativism, by abuse, by generational curses, by unfaithfulness, by poverty, by abandonment. If you do not take time for your children, to pray over them and speak into their lives, they won't stand a fighting chance.

Psalm 78:9 is a sobering Scripture: "The children of Ephraim, being armed and carrying bows, turned back in the day of battle." Can you imagine going into battle armed with bows but no arrows? You'd get crushed! As a parent, you cannot fight the good fight of faith against the forces of darkness with a bow and an empty quiver. You won't win. This is why you've got to be relentless about digging the well of sacrifice, the well of discipline, the well of quality time and the well of faithfulness. When we point our children in the right direction, our children will be the weapons God will use to stop the enemy.

God is trying to raise an army, a family. Our families are supposed to terrify the enemy. "As for me and my house, we will serve the LORD" (Joshua 24:15). If we commit to raising and nurturing a godly family, our children will charge the gates of hell. We will reap acres of diamonds of what is possible when God works in and through them. So equip your children. Pray for them. Take them to church. Read the Bible with them. Have discussions about faith. Restore the broken arrows and unleash them into the world for Jesus. They will uncover acres of diamonds far greater than they could ever imagine.

Ricky Hoyt was born a spastic quadriplegic with cerebral palsy, unable to walk or talk as he grew. Doctors told his parents their son would be little more than a vegetable and suggested institutionalizing him. Ricky's parents refused. They began to work with him, teaching him to read. When he was eleven, Ricky learned to communicate with a computer and started attending public school. He went on to university and eventually worked for Boston College. When Ricky was fifteen, he heard about a race to support an athlete from his school who had become paralyzed. He told his father, Dick, about it. Dick was a non-runner. He had zero desire to run, but seeing how badly his son wanted to participate, he figured out a way. He would run and push his son in a wheelchair across the finish line. After this first race, Rick told his father, "When I'm running, it feels like I'm not handicapped."[3] Dick began training hard-core and entering more races, all for his son. It was the beginning of an incredible sports endurance father-and-son team that has competed in 1,130 endurance events, including 72 marathons, 6 full-distance triathlons (the Ironman distance), and 7 half-distance triathlons.

I think of this earthly father and am reminded how we are totally incapable of making it to the finish line without our heavenly Father. The enemy wants to destroy you and your marriage, giving him a clear path to then destroy your children. He does not want you to see the acres of diamonds in your home. He is in hot pursuit to rob you of these things. It's not easy being married. It's not easy raising a family. But Jesus will push you through every rocky road. He will push you over every mountain. He will push you through every ocean. He will push you through every obstacle. And He will get you across the finish line.

If you aren't already, start digging wells for you and your family. And instead of fighting with your spouse or your kids, start fighting for your family. His grace is sufficient to bring out the diamonds of victory over strife, bitterness, infidelity, bickering and unforgiveness.

❖ 11 ❖

If You're in It, You Can Win It

When the people of Israel left Egypt, God led them not through the land of the Philistines but around it, by way of the wilderness.[1] He did this on purpose. He knew had they gone the first route, they would have gotten into conflict with the Philistines, become discouraged and returned to Egypt. Because the people of Israel were not ready to face the enemy, God took them the long way around.

There is a foundational truth here. This Scripture tells me if we are in a tough spot, God has either put us there or has allowed us to be there. And if we're in it, we can win it.

Conflict builds strength. A lot of times our prayers revolve around telling God to get us out of something. But He has you where you are for a reason. There are times when God wants to do something for you, and then there are times when He wants to do something through you.

Are you going through a conflict in your life right now? Are you struggling with an addiction, with bitterness from something that happened, with an injustice, a health issue or turmoil within your marriage or your family? I want to give you good news: God has already equipped you to win. If your situation seems impossible right now, know that God is the God of the impossible. No matter how devastating your current situation, you, right now, are standing on top of acres of diamonds. He is your victory.

Great Victories among Dry Bones

Jesus challenged His disciples with this simple exhortation: "Nothing will be impossible for you" (Matthew 17:20). When God asks you to do something possible and you do it, it makes you look good. But when God gives you something impossible to do (or an impossible place to stay in), and then He uses you to do it, He looks good!

I think the adventure we all signed up for the day we declared Jesus to be Lord of our lives was about doing the impossible. The person armed with faith is more powerful than the person who has all the facts. The facts are real, but the truth is greater than the facts. The facts may say, "You do not have enough money to do what God is calling you to do." But the truth says, "God will meet all your needs according to His riches in glory!"

It may feel impossible to look at your situation and see acres of diamonds, but I bet you have never been presented with as big an impossibility as the ancient prophet Ezekiel. As Ezekiel 37 records, he found himself in a large valley, a low place. When he looked around, as far as his eyes could see, the ground was littered with piles of human bones that were disjointed and cracked in the sun. God asked Ezekiel if the bones could live. The prophet wisely answered, "O Lord God, You know" (verse 3). In other words, Ezekiel had no clue how it could happen, but He trusted that God would know.

The situation must have looked utterly hopeless to the natural eye. But the Lord had a plan. He told Ezekiel to prophesy to the bones. I believe this passage beautifully illustrates the power of the breath of God, how He brings life into dead situations. The valley that was strewn with bones became alive. And out of it emerged a living and breathing army, powered by the very breath of God that brings life out of death and hope out of hopelessness. Acres of diamonds!

The enemy may have wrapped a rope of hopelessness around your life to the point that you feel that you cannot take another breath. Be encouraged. The same breath of God that brought Adam to life also brought Ezekiel's dry bones to life, breathed the Holy Spirit into the disciples in the Upper Room and inspired every word of the Bible.

You may be standing in a graveyard in some area of your life. Maybe your marriage is dead. Maybe your finances are dead. Maybe your career is fading. Maybe your dream has failed. Well, you are in a good place, because the greatest victory ever won was won in a graveyard!

Your greatest victory comes when it seems as though everything around you is dead. It's easy to lose your joy when you cannot see the acres of diamonds where God has called you to stay. It's human nature. When we get in a valley, the enemy wants to dry up our joy. But I refuse to let a sinner have more fun in his sin than I am going to have in my righteousness through Christ Jesus! Do not let the devil dry you up. Do not become insecure or discouraged just because your circumstances look different than what you believe God has promised you. Instead, stir up your joy. If the

The greatest victory ever won was won in a graveyard!

hand of the Lord takes you into a low place, remember that the joy of the Lord is your strength (see Nehemiah 8:10). Strengthen yourself in Him when you are in a valley. Pray. Meditate on His Word. Surround yourself with people who will encourage you.

One more thing—get your eyes off the dead bones. Don't focus all your attention, energy and time on your current graveyard situation. Focus on the fact that God has a purpose for your life and a purpose for where you are. Stay in that place. God can bring to life something that was dead. That dream. That marriage. That calling. The only thing alive in the valley of dry bones was Ezekiel. You may be the very one God has chosen to bring life to something that is dead right now. You may be the instrument of revival.

You know what our problem is? We pray for rain and leave our umbrella at home. We lack faith that God can do the impossible. When God is ready for you to do something, sometimes He may just throw you where He wants you to go. You may not know why you are there. You may not even understand what is going on. There is no telling where God is about to throw you.

Do not mistake your battleground for a graveyard. The reason those bones were not buried is because God was not through with them. You are not in a graveyard. You are in a battleground. And God will win the war.

Get Under God's Hand

One of the greatest prayers we need to begin to pray is for the hand of the Lord to come upon us. When the hand of the Lord is upon us, we can do what others cannot. Regardless of where we are in the natural, things can happen to us that exceed our greatest expectations, but only if the hand of the Lord is upon us.

Ezekiel experienced the miracle of the dry bones coming alive because "the hand of the LORD came upon me and brought me out in the Spirit of the LORD."[2] We need the hand of God on our lives, especially when we seem to have been planted in a barren wasteland. You can climb to the top of the corporate ladder, own homes on multiple continents and have a bank account a king would be proud of, but without the anointing that comes from walking in communion with God, it is all for nothing. When we invite God to cover our efforts with His Spirit, we cannot fail! It is impossible! He is the difference maker. He is the sustaining one. The fulfiller. The promoter. The comforter. The healer. Our ever present help in times of need.

This anointing is found in only one place—the hand of the Lord. We can see from the Bible just how significant it is. Acts 11:21 tells us that "the hand of the Lord was with them, and a great number believed and turned to the Lord."

I used to think this was a strange phrase. Why did it say that "the hand of the Lord was with them" rather than just "the Lord was with them"? When I started studying this phrase—"the hand of the Lord"—I found it over and over in the Bible. (Rather than inundating you with Scripture references, when you get a free moment, do a search and see for yourself. It's pretty amazing!) When I was growing up in the church, we dealt with some big problems too difficult to solve with our natural wisdom and ability. The old-timers in the church would always say, "Let's just put it in the hands of God." There is more to that than even they probably realized.

One of my favorite Scriptures on this topic is the prayer that Jabez prayed: "Oh, that You would bless me indeed, and enlarge my territory, that Your hand would be with me, and that You would keep me from evil, that I may not cause pain!" (1 Chronicles 4:10). The hand of the Lord is powerful. Jabez knew this. We should, too. Regardless of what the present situation looks like, when the hand of the Lord comes upon us and we get in sync with the Holy Spirit, everything changes. Maybe not our circumstance in that very moment, but God develops in us what we need to carry out our purpose through it.

When the hand of the Lord is upon you, you can do what others cannot do. You have protection. It upholds you. You have courage. You have a vision and will not be distracted. You succeed. You sleep in peace. You have joy unspeakable. No weapon formed against you will prosper (including your own stupidity). When the hand of the Lord is upon you, nobody can do anything about it. More than praying for God to change circumstances in our favor, we need to pray for His hand to be on our lives. This is the only way to uncover acres of diamonds.

The enemy would love nothing more than for you to back up right now instead of staying put and uncovering acres of diamonds. He wants you to give up. He wants you to move from the place or the people to whom God has called you. He wants you to think your situation is impossible. Know that God is faithful to complete what He started (see Philippians 1:6). He will finish the work that He has started in your life.

Often we think that the world's definition of success is what matters. That our testimony is showing those who don't know Jesus how well off we are or how far we've come materially speaking. What's important, however, is to show the world the touch of God on our lives and our families. Natural diamonds fade, but spiritual diamonds—the hidden treasures of God—are eternal.

We didn't have much growing up in Henderson, North Carolina. Our family lived by a cotton mill. In addition to his job as a pastor, my dad sold sandwiches. He would get up around four in the morning, pack a hundred or so aluminum foil–wrapped sausage biscuit sandwiches that Mom made into his dusty old pickup truck, and head down to the mill to sell them for a quarter or fifty cents apiece. He didn't make much money, but he made enough to support our family. We didn't have nice cars. We lived in a little house. We didn't have the newest or best of anything. What we did have, though, was priceless and eternal and made the biggest difference. We had the hand of God over us. There was something about the prayers of my parents that settled His hand over our lives. We kids knew it, and we could never shake it.

When God's hand is upon you in situations that are impossible, He will bring you opportunities in which He will show up and show off.

When President Donald Trump took office, I was invited to be part of the Presidential Evangelical Advisory Committee, and I accepted. Whatever political opinions you have about the man or the office, I want to say that I've learned that presence is everything. I believe God called me to this role. I may not agree with everything President Trump says or does, but I cannot influence him if I am not at the table. And I've taken criticism for being at the table. I've taken attack after attack. But I've stayed in that place, no matter how badly the critics and naysayers lash out against me.

In 2018, I was in a meeting at the White House in Washington, D.C., in which I spoke about the DACA (Deferred Action for Childhood Arrivals) policy. This policy allows children of immigrants who came into the country illegally to remain here if they were younger than sixteen when they arrived, provided they had lived in the United States since 2007. We call these children Dreamers. When I spoke at this meeting, the DACA program was at risk of being eliminated. As a follower of Christ, I believe our laws should always be undergirded by both justice and mercy. In the case of Dreamers, these values couldn't be more applicable. They were brought to America not of their own accord. They had no choice but to grow up here. I don't think anyone can blame them for building a life here. Dreamers are in my church, they're in my life, they're friends with my children and they're my friends. I care about these kids and believe they should have the opportunity for a proper pathway to citizenship.

In supporting the cause of Dreamers, my speech caught the attention of the President. Within five minutes, I found myself in an unbelievable situation, something that could only be attributed to the hand of God over my life. I was quickly ushered into the Oval Office and sat down in front of the President's desk. How did a preacher's kid from a small town in the middle of nowhere end up here? I didn't put myself here. I didn't ask for this. It was the hand of the Lord. The God of the impossible.

Next thing I knew, I was at the table with President Trump. He walked into the office, sat across from me at his desk and looked me in the eye. For seven minutes we discussed DACA and Dreamers, and I was able to speak into the situation. I do not know what the outcome will be, but I do know that without the hand of God over my life, I would not have had the opportunity to make a difference in the place where He has called me.

Since that time I have been to the White House and have met with President Trump and his administration numerous times. It has been a tremendous honor to give him the Christian perspective on a variety of issues such as abortion, Israel policy, prison reform and urban renewal. I have witnessed things in some of these meetings that only the hand of the Lord could have orchestrated.

When the hand of the Lord is upon your life, it's not about uncovering acres of diamonds for your purpose, enjoyment or glory. It's about Him. It's about His purpose. It's about His agenda.

Say It

We fight for the fullness of God's blessing for ourselves and our families by engaging the prophetic word in our spiritual battles.

The apostle Paul gave a certain instruction to Timothy, his co-worker in spreading the Gospel and establishing multiple churches:

> This charge I commit to you, son Timothy, according to the prophecies previously made concerning you, that by them you may wage the good warfare, having faith and a good conscience, which some having rejected, concerning the faith have suffered shipwreck.
>
> 1 Timothy 1:18–19

I love the fact that Paul connects this instruction with prophecy. He tells Timothy to go to war, to engage in spiritual warfare with prophecies. The Passion Translation puts it this way: "Use your prophecies as weapons as you wage spiritual warfare by faith and with a clean conscience."

Prophecy is a word from God about your future. It's not about where you are; it's about where you will be. Where you are may look nothing like acres of diamonds, but you have faith that one day it will. Though there are a number of ways God speaks to us, the most obvious is through the Bible. The Word of God is full of promises that we can use to prophesy over our lives.

You have a prophecy over your life. Now, this is important— while God will always keep His promises, He is not obligated to keep our potential. When He speaks a word of prophecy over our lives, it is our responsibility to take that word and go to war with it. In Timothy's case, Paul told him to take the prophecies and wage spiritual warfare against any and every thing that tried

181

to stop him from walking into the future that God had for him. The same is true for you today. If you are going to walk into the prophecy over your life, you are required to engage in a spiritual war. You don't automatically step into it. It requires a fight.

Notice Paul tells Timothy to wage war having faith and a good conscience. A good, or clean, conscience is connected to strong faith. A defiled conscience weakens our faith. Living right creates a clean conscience, and that creates strong faith. Treasure and protect a clean conscience. This is one of the greatest things you have to build your faith. Without faith, you will lose the battle.

Speak Spiritual Blessing into Existence

We receive some spiritual gifts by inheritance. Jesus said that unless we receive the Kingdom of God as a child, we cannot enter it (see Mark 10:15). What does this mean? There are things in the Kingdom that we cannot earn. We can't perform well enough to get them. We don't deserve them. But Jesus said that because we are children of God, we can enter the Kingdom of God and therefore receive our spiritual inheritance. Because our identity is in Jesus, we receive the gifts of salvation, forgiveness, grace and eternal life. His blood has been given to us. We are bone of His bone, flesh of His flesh.

In Matthew 11:12, Jesus talks about how the Kingdom of heaven suffers violence and the violent take it by force. While we receive some things through our spiritual inheritance, there are other blessings, like the fullness of prophecy, that we have to learn how to take by force, spiritually speaking.

Let me give you an example. If you have a family, the Bible offers a prophecy for them. "As for me and my house, we will serve the LORD."[3] Now, it's not enough for you to just read it and leave it hanging. You are responsible for stewarding that prophecy.

If you are looking to uncover acres of diamonds in your family, if it seems no one besides you is serving God, you are to take this weapon of prophecy and go to war with it. When the enemy comes to destroy you and your family, enter into spiritual warfare with this promise.

The Word of God will get you where the will of God wants to take you. But you have to say it. You have to speak it. You have to declare it. You have to pray it. You have to decree it. It's up to you to take a prophetic word and go to war with that prophecy. Something has to be spoken. It is time to start decreeing the Word of God over your life.

You have to talk to mountains. You have to talk to lies. You have to talk to sin. You have to talk to addiction. You have to talk to demons. You have to go to war with prophecy. Pray and say it until it happens. Even today, right now, start saying things like this:

Lack is not my prophecy. I have more than enough.

Defeat and addiction are not my prophecy. I am overcoming by the blood of the Lamb.

A messed-up family is not my prophecy. We will serve the Lord.

One proclamation of the Word of God in some area of your life can make a profound difference. The weapons of prophecy will take you and your family into places you can't take them into.

God told Jeremiah that He watches over His Word to perform it.[4] The most powerful prayer that you can pray is when you tell Him what He's already said to you in His Word. When you do this, you remind God of His promises. This is exactly what Daniel did. We read in the Bible that he waged war in prayer with a prophecy found in Jeremiah that predicted the end of Israel's seventy-year captivity. "I've been looking in my calendar," Daniel prayed. "Today is seventy years. What are you going to do about the prophecy that's been hanging over my head?"[5] And God broke the captivity and reestablished the nation of Israel.

The Word of God will get you where the will of God wants to take you. But you have to say it. You have to speak it. You have to declare it. You have to pray it. You have to decree it.

Some of you quit too soon. It does not matter how long you've been fighting. If the prophecy has not yet come to pass, if you have not yet uncovered acres of diamonds, keep waging the good fight. Stay in the battlefield. God will bring victory sooner or later.

The power of life and death are in the tongue. Speak because you serve the God of the impossible. Speak because nothing happens in the spirit world until you open your mouth and say it. Start today and speak life to your dreams. Speak life to your calling. Speak life to your children. Speak life to your body. Speak life to your children's destiny. Speak life to the low places. Prophesy that the sun is going to shine again. Prophesy that you will see the goodness of the Lord while you are still alive. Prophesy that plenty will be your place again. It may have been bad, but prophesy that you are coming out of it. Prophesy that you are about to turn the corner on your miracle. You may have had a setback, you may have messed up, but God is not through with you yet.

Pray today, not for God to give you words to comfort you or ones in which you will find rest, but for Him to give you fresh words to fight with.

❖ 12 ❖

Heaven, the Ultimate Acres of Diamonds

C. S. Lewis wrote,

If you read history you will find that the Christians who did most for the present world were just those who thought most of the next. The Apostles themselves, who set on foot the conversion of the Roman Empire, the great men who built up the Middle Ages, the English Evangelicals who abolished the Slave Trade, all left their mark on Earth, precisely because their minds were occupied with Heaven. It is since Christians have largely ceased to think of the other world that they have become so ineffective in this.[1]

We cannot only focus on the acres of diamonds that are uncovered in this life. We must focus on the big picture. We need to have heaven on our mind. This world is not our home; we are just pilgrims passing through. When you have been through the heat and the pressure and the fire of life and feel like you have nothing left, I want to remind you of the greatest acres of diamonds you will ever find—eternal life with God in heaven.

How long is eternity? Forever and forever. There was a time when you were not, but there will never be a time when you will not be. When Caesar ruled Rome, you were not. When Columbus sailed the world, you were not. When the Founding Fathers established America, you were not. But there will never be a day from now on when you will not be somewhere.

Your mind probably cannot grasp the truth that in a million years, five million years, a billion years from now, your soul will be alive somewhere. If you love and serve Jesus, your last breath here on earth will be your first breath in heaven forever and ever. Oh, I hope this encourages you as much as it does me.

When you are strained and stretched to your limits emotionally, hounded by physical pain, harassed by financial difficulty or overwhelmed by relationship conflict, it is easy to keep your attention on these things. This is what the enemy wants us to do—focus on our problems and not on God's promises. He wants us to live shallow, earth-bound lives. He wants our attention fixed on the temporal and not the eternal, because we become dangerous to his plans when we have eternity in our sight.

Heaven Is Real

The promise of heaven is real. We are going to stand on those streets of gold one day. We are going to hug everyone we love who arrived there before us. We are going to dance in the presence of Jesus. It's real. And it's waiting for us. This world is not our final destination. It's not our true home. Our home is with our Father in heaven.

There is a story about a little boy who was born blind. He had never seen his mother's face. He had never seen the beauties of nature. He had never seen a sunset. He had never seen a flower.

He had never seen snow. Over the years, his mother had tried her best to describe these things to him. One day, she heard about a renowned doctor who could perform a surgery that gave those who were blind their sight. She took her son for a consultation, and her son was approved for surgery. The operation was successful. After a period of recovery, it was time for the boy to have the bandages that had covered his eyes since the surgery removed. When the final one was unwrapped, it took a second or two for the boy to focus. Suddenly, he ran to the window and gasped. Golden sunshine illuminated the sparkling blue sky. The grass was vibrant green and the flowers draped with such colors!

His eyes wide, the boy turned to his mother and said, "Oh, Mother, why didn't you tell me I was living in such a beautiful world?"

With tears falling down her cheeks, she replied, "Sweetheart, I tried. I just couldn't do it justice!"

This is the same sentiment Paul felt when he tried to describe the wonder and beauty of heaven. "Eye has not seen, nor ear heard, nor have entered into the heart of man the things which God has prepared for those who love Him" (1 Corinthians 2:9).

Jesus said,

> Let not your heart be troubled; you believe in God, believe also in Me. In My Father's house are many mansions; if it were not so, I would have told you. I go to prepare a place for you. And if I go and prepare a place for you, I will come again and receive you to Myself; that where I am, there you may be also. And where I go you know, and the way you know.
>
> John 14:1–4

Jesus didn't leave this earth to prepare just any place for those who believe in Him. Heaven is more spectacular than we can imagine. The foundation is built with twelve layers of precious stones. It has streets of fine-spun gold. A river of life. Mansions created by the architect of the ages. My mansion is there. Yours is, too.

It is said that the Roman emperor Domitian had the apostle John thrown into a pot of boiling oil. Miraculously, he escaped unharmed. God did not appoint him to die, for John still had an assignment left on earth: to write the book of Revelation. In an effort to be rid of John, Domitian banished him to an island called Patmos. It was there that God allowed John to see a door from which He said (my paraphrase), "Hey, John, you having a bad day? A bad week? Come up here. Come see from heaven's perspective what's really going on when you're having a bad day down there."[2]

When God said, "Come up," John was able to enter paradise, to peer into heaven. Heaven is a place, you see. It's real. It's not a state of mind. It's not a sentimental dream. It's not a figment of our imagination that we make up to comfort people who are grieving the loss of a loved one. John wrote,

> Now I saw a new heaven and a new earth, for the first heaven and the first earth had passed away. Also there was no more sea. Then I, John, saw the holy city, New Jerusalem, coming down out of heaven from God, prepared as a bride adorned for her husband. And I heard a loud voice from heaven saying, "Behold, the tabernacle of God is with men, and He will dwell with them, and they shall be His people. God Himself will be with them and be their God."
>
> Revelation 21:1–3

Heaven is mentioned in 54 of the 66 books of the Bible. In the book of Matthew alone, Jesus mentions it 70 times. If heaven is not real, then the Bible is a lie.

When Jesus was ascending into heaven after His death and resurrection, His disciples stood awestruck, staring after His dramatic exit. Suddenly, two angels appeared alongside them. "Men of Galilee, why do you stand gazing up into heaven?" they asked the disciples. "This same Jesus, who was taken up from you into heaven, will so come in like manner as you saw Him go into heaven" (Acts 1:11).

Paul wrote,

For the Lord Himself will descend from heaven with a shout, with the voice of an archangel, and with the trumpet of God. And the dead in Christ will rise first. Then we who are alive and remain shall be caught up together with them in the clouds to meet the Lord in the air. And thus we shall always be with the Lord. Therefore comfort one another with these words.

1 Thessalonians 4:16–18

Notice the last line: *Comfort one another with these words*. We are commanded to preach about heaven. We are commanded to talk about the rapture of the Church of Jesus Christ. Jesus did not want His people only thinking about earth. He wanted them to know that there is more to this life on earth—and to live with that in mind.

Life is hard. Trials sway us. Problems come and go. The struggle is real. But so is heaven. This should fill us with joy and hope. No matter what happens in this life, those who believe in Jesus will receive God's ultimate blessing, His best gift for us—eternal life with Him in heaven. Acres and acres and acres of diamonds!

When I was growing up in my dad's little country church, I did everything in our music department. I played the drums. I played the sax. I played the piano. I led the adult choir. I led the children's choir. I sang the solos. One of the songs that we often sang talked about how we're feeling mighty fine because heaven is on our mind, and how we want to go where the milk and honey flow, and so forth. When we sang that song, the church would go wild. The drums would pound through the walls. The organ would echo down the street. People would dance and shout in the aisles. I loved it because it reminded me that heaven was real and I would go there one day.

No matter what happens in this life, those who believe in Jesus will receive God's ultimate blessing, His best gift for us—eternal life with Him in heaven.

If you want to get from place to place in our solar system, you travel at the speed of light, which is about 670 million miles per hour. To get from the sun to the planet Mercury (a distance of 35.98 million miles) would take 3.2 minutes at light speed. A trip from the sun to earth (92.96 million miles) would take 8.5 minutes. From the sun to Neptune (2.79 billion miles), 4.3 hours.

You could travel past all of these places and still not reach heaven. But when God told John to come up here and see heaven, the Bible says that "immediately" he was there (see Revelation 4:2). Can you imagine? Faster than the speed of light! In the twinkling of an eye, we will be changed. We will leave behind this earth and be in the presence of the Lord in the heavenly realm. Death will be swallowed up in victory.

All Things Made New

Life on this earth is hard. But as believers, we have the hope of eternity stored up in us. "God will wipe away every tear from their eyes; there shall be no more death, nor sorrow, nor crying. There shall be no more pain" (Revelation 21:4).

Heaven is a place of life.

Envision right now the most beautiful place you have ever been to. Maybe it's a tropical paradise with a crystal clear beach, swaying palm trees, warm sunlight beaming on your face. Maybe it's a majestic mountain scene, a rushing waterfall tumbling over jagged rocks. Maybe it's a landscape of glorious autumn aspen on a hillside lit by the glowing light of the dawn.

Think of your friends and your family who loved Jesus and have gone on before you. They're running to you with open arms. Picture them as you're walking together in this beautiful place. You're laughing. You're playing. You're talking. You're reminiscing. You're hugging. But someone is coming. It's Jesus. He has a big smile on His face. See yourself falling to your knees. As He pulls you up and embraces you, He says with a smile as bright as the sun, "Welcome home." You have entered into the joy of the Lord. What a glorious day!

In heaven, the old things of earth are gone. Everything is new. You feel God's love and His peace permeating the place. You are completely and totally at home and deeply satisfied. It is the place you have always looked for on earth but never found. And you finally realize that this marvelous place made every trial, every heartache and every pain you experienced on earth worth it.

Heaven is a place of rejoicing. Hundreds of thousands of angels, living creatures and elders gather around the throne of God and worship Him.[3]

Heaven is also a place of reunion. Our loved ones on earth are separated by death, separated by sorrow, separated by tragedy; but when we all get to heaven, what a day of rejoicing it will be. I'm often asked if we will know each other in heaven. The answer is yes! Paul wrote that in heaven, the whole family of God is there.[4] He also wrote, "For now we see in a mirror, dimly, but then face to face. Now I know in part, but then I shall know just as I also am known" (1 Corinthians 13:12). When Jesus was on the Mount of Transfiguration with Peter, James and John, they knew Moses and Elijah, who appeared before them. Yes! We will know our loved ones who believed in Jesus and who have gone before us.

When Jesus was on earth, Mary saw Him as her baby in a manger in Bethlehem. John the Baptist saw Him as the candidate for baptism. The disciples saw Him as a rabbi and master teacher. Rome saw Him as an insurrectionist. The citizens saw Him as a common thief. And the religious leaders saw Him as a drunkard, a liar and a heretic. But when we get to heaven, we shall see Jesus as He is, and we shall know Him.[5] We shall see Him as the Lord of glory. We shall see Him high and lifted up. We shall see Him as the Alpha and the Omega. We shall see Him as the Lamb of God, the light of the world, the Lion of the tribe of Judah, the fairest of ten thousand, the bright and morning star. We shall see Him as heaven's hope and hell's defeat. We shall see Him as the great I Am, the great physician, the great shepherd, my rock, my fortress, my high tower, the King of kings and the Lord of lords. We shall see Him face to face! Let this encourage you!

I have talked a lot about what awaits us in heaven. Now let me tell you what will not be in heaven.

There will be no funeral homes in heaven. There will be no hospitals. There will be no divorce courts. There will be no bankruptcy courts. There will be no addiction centers. There will be no teen suicide. There will be no pornography. There will be no cancer. There will be no rape. There will be no missing children. There will be no drug problems. There will be no gangs. There will be no shootings. There will be no acts of terrorism.

There will be no racial tensions or racial divide in heaven. There will be no prejudice. There will be no injustice. There will be no misunderstandings. There will be no harsh words. There will be no hurt feelings. There will be no arguments. There will be no eating disorders. There will be no jealousy. There will be no rage. There will be no gossip. There will be no worry. There will be no depression. There will be no child abuse. There will be no wars. There will be no emotional breakdowns. There will be no murders. There will be no trials, no trauma, no temptations.

There will be no heart monitors. There will be no wheelchairs. There will be no rust. There will be no bad habits. There will be no locked doors. There will be no sin. There will be no accidents. There will be no suffering. There will be no separation. There will be no starvation. There will be no tears, because He is going to wipe every tear from our eyes. No sorrow. No sickness. No death. No pain.

The Bible mentions there will be no more sea.[6] This doesn't mean there won't be beautiful bodies of water. There's a deeper meaning to the word *sea* here. It may sound like a strange statement, but in ancient days the sea represented separation and storms. The sea separated people from families and was associated with raging weather. In other words, in heaven, there will be no more separation from our loved ones, and we will not see another storm for all eternity.

These are the glorious acres of diamonds that await all of us who believe in Jesus. The old, the broken, the ugly, the failure, the sin is gone. In heaven, all things are made new. We will have new names, new bodies, new homes and new natures. We will live in a new city, drink new wine and sing a new song. All things are made new!

Work Now for an Eternal Reward

This is why we ought to "be steadfast, immovable, always abounding in the work of the Lord, knowing that your labor is not in vain in the Lord" (1 Corinthians 15:58). Get heaven on your mind.

Know that Jesus is coming back, and your reward is with Him. What we are doing on this earth is not in vain. Your prayers are not in vain. Your fasting is not in vain. Your standing on the Word is not in vain. Your trials, trouble and pain are not in vain.

Take comfort in how Paul explains it:

> For our light affliction, which is but for a moment, is working for us a far more exceeding and eternal weight of glory, while we do not look at the things which are seen, but at the things which are not seen. For the things which are seen are temporary, but the things which are not seen are eternal.
>
> 2 Corinthians 4:17–18

When you get your mind on heaven, you will see your situation on earth in a new light.

My word to you is "Work now." Now is the time. If you have a soul to win, win it now. If you have a song to sing, sing it now. If you have a prayer to pray, pray it now. If you have a person to encourage, encourage him or her now. Don't live for pleasure. Don't live for things that temporarily satisfy. Live for Jesus today. The time is now.

Heaven is not a fairy tale. Heaven is a real place filled with wonders beyond what we can even begin to imagine. If you try to think of the greatest, most joy-filled and pleasurable place, it will not come close to what heaven will actually be like. God loves you. He prepared heaven for you, and He wants you to spend eternity there. Maybe you don't get rewarded much here on earth, but I promise you a day of reward in heaven is coming.

Jesus said, "Rejoice and be exceedingly glad, for great is your reward in heaven, for so they persecuted the prophets who were before you" (Matthew 5:12). You may not feel appreciated or valued on earth. Don't worry about it. Your reward is not here. Your reward is in heaven. "Behold, I am coming quickly, and My reward is with Me, to give to every one according to his work" (Revelation 22:12).

What kind of reward will you get in heaven? The Bible gives us a glimpse:

> "Let us be glad and rejoice and give Him glory, for the marriage of the Lamb has come, and His wife has made herself ready." And to her it was granted to be arrayed in fine linen, clean and bright, for the fine linen is the righteous acts of the saints.
>
> Revelation 19:7–8

Your garment will be constructed by your righteous acts, what you do on earth, how you live for Jesus now. Some of you will have a beautiful gown at the marriage supper, and some of you will just have enough linen for a pair of socks. Your service to God here will determine your quality of reward there.

It is easy to forget why God saved you, what He has called you to do and how you are supposed to live. So here's a memo from heaven to help you live today while setting your mind on eternity:

> Don't just pretend to love others. Really love them. Hate what is wrong. Hold tightly to what is good. Love each other with genuine affection, and take delight in honoring each other. Never be lazy, but work hard and serve the Lord enthusiastically.
>
> Rejoice in our confident hope. Be patient in trouble, and keep on praying. When God's people are in need, be ready to help them. Always be eager to practice hospitality.
>
> Bless those who persecute you. Don't curse them; pray that God will bless them. Be happy with those who are happy, and weep with those who weep. Live in harmony with each other. Don't be too proud to enjoy the company of ordinary people. And don't think you know it all!

Never pay back evil with more evil. Do things in such a way that everyone can see you are honorable. Do all that you can to live in peace with everyone.

Dear friends, never take revenge. Leave that to the righteous anger of God. For the Scriptures say, "I will take revenge; I will pay them back," says the LORD. Instead, "If your enemies are hungry, feed them. If they are thirsty, give them something to drink. In doing this, you will heap burning coals of shame on their heads." Don't let evil conquer you, but conquer evil by doing good.

Romans 12:9–21 NLT

If you are not sure if you will live for eternity in heaven, I am going to give you an opportunity to say a prayer. You don't get to heaven by accident. It's by appointment only. Make your appointment sure. Choose today who you will serve.

If you do not have peace with God, if you're not living right and want to surrender your life to Jesus, I invite you to pray this prayer out loud:

In Your mighty name, Jesus, I believe that You died on Calvary and shed Your blood so that I could be forgiven. Today, right now, I receive You as my Lord and Savior. I, by faith, refuse that which is evil, and I receive Your will for my life. Thank You, Jesus, for Your precious blood that cleanses me. I am forgiven and my name is written in the Book of Life. I will spend eternity in heaven, in Jesus' mighty name. Amen.

If you just prayed this prayer, welcome to the family of God! Starting today, humble yourself, take up your cross and follow Jesus until He calls you to your eternal home in heaven.

We need to stand on the promise of heaven. If you are having a bad day, do what Jesus said to John: Come up here. You're invited. You're welcome in this place.

If you are going through something bleak on earth, come up here and you'll see a whole new perspective.

Whether things are going well or falling apart, come up here and take a glimpse of what God has in store for you.

One day you'll truly be home forever—because heaven, the ultimate acres of diamonds, is real and waiting for you.

Wherever you are in this very moment, God is waiting to open your eyes to the wondrous things He has for you. All you have to do is ask Him and trust Him. Remember, acres of diamonds are uncovered in unusual places. Usually, where you are right now. If you look close with spiritual eyes, you will find much hidden potential and untapped opportunity lying in the field right under your feet.

So stay in the place where you are right now. Don't worry about what tomorrow will bring, and stop living in regret of what you did or didn't do yesterday. Your joy, your purpose, your peace and your hope are here, now. If the grass on the other side looks greener than the grass you are standing on, fertilize your lawn. Start digging in your own backyard and watch as God unfolds diamonds in what you may think is a valley of dry bones.

One day you'll truly be home forever—because heaven, the ultimate acres of diamonds, is real and waiting for you.

The time is now to lay hold of your acres of diamonds. He is waiting for you to let down your bucket and pull up refreshing water for your soul. He is waiting to quench your thirst and charge your spirit. He is waiting for you to find life, growth, strength and peace. It's here, now.

What are you waiting for?

Appendix

Acres of Diamonds

by Russell H. Conwell[1]

This lecture has been delivered under these circumstances: I visit a town or city, and try to arrive there early enough to see the postmaster, the barber, the keeper of the hotel, the principal of the schools and the ministers of some of the churches, and then go into some of the factories and stores and talk with the people, and get into sympathy with the local conditions of that town or city and see what has been their history, what opportunities they had and what they had failed to do—and every town fails to do something—and then go to the lecture and talk to those people about the subjects which applied to their locality. "Acres of Diamonds"—the idea—has continuously been precisely the same. The idea is that in this country of ours every man has the opportunity to make more of himself than he does in his own environment, with his own skill, with his own energy and with his own friends.

Russell H. Conwell

When going down the Tigris and Euphrates rivers many years ago with a party of English travelers, I found myself under the direction of an old Arab guide whom we hired up at Bagdad [*sic*], and I have often thought how that guide resembled our barbers in certain mental characteristics. He thought that it was not only his duty to guide us down those rivers, and do what he was paid for doing, but also to entertain us with stories curious and weird, ancient and modern, strange and familiar. Many of them I have forgotten, and I am glad I have, but there is one I shall never forget.

The old guide was leading my camel by its halter along the banks of those ancient rivers, and he told me story after story until I grew weary of his storytelling and ceased to listen. I have never been irritated with that guide when he lost his temper as I ceased listening. But I remember that he took off his Turkish cap and swung it in a circle to get my attention. I could see it through the corner of my eye, but I determined not to look straight at him for fear he would tell another story. But although I am not a woman, I did finally look, and as soon as I did he went right into another story.

Said he, "I will tell you a story now which I reserve for my particular friends." When he emphasized the words "particular friends," I listened, and I have ever been glad I did. I really feel devoutly thankful, that there are 1,674 young men who have been carried through college by this lecture who are also glad that I did listen. The old guide told me that there once lived not far from the river Indus an ancient Persian by the name of Ali Hafed. He said that Ali Hafed owned a very large farm, that he had orchards, grain fields and gardens; that he had money at interest and was a wealthy and contented man. He was contented because he was wealthy, and wealthy because he was contented. One day there visited that old Persian farmer one of those ancient Buddhist priests, one of the wise men of the East. He sat down by the fire and told the old farmer how this world of ours was made. He said that this world was once a mere bank of fog, and that the Almighty thrust His finger into this bank of fog and began slowly to move His finger around, increasing the speed until at last He whirled this bank of fog into a solid ball of fire. Then it went rolling through the universe, burning its way through other banks of fog, and condensed the moisture without, until it fell in floods of rain upon its hot surface and cooled the outward crust. Then the internal fires bursting outward through the crust threw up the mountains and hills, the valleys, the plains and prairies of this wonderful world of ours. If this internal molten mass came bursting out and cooled very quickly it became granite; less quickly copper, less quickly silver, less quickly gold, and, after gold, diamonds were made.

Said the old priest, "A diamond is a congealed drop of sunlight." Now that is literally scientifically true, that a diamond is an actual deposit of carbon from the sun. The old priest told Ali Hafed that if he had one diamond the size of his thumb he could purchase the county, and if he had a mine of diamonds he could place his children upon thrones through the influence of their great wealth.

Ali Hafed heard all about diamonds, how much they were worth, and went to his bed that night a poor man. He had not lost anything, but he was poor because he was discontented, and discontented because he feared he was poor. He said, "I want a mine of diamonds," and he lay awake all night.

Early in the morning he sought out the priest. I know by experience that a priest is very cross when awakened early in the morning, and when he shook that old priest out of his dreams, Ali Hafed said to him:

"Will you tell me where I can find diamonds?"

"Diamonds! What do you want with diamonds?"

"Why, I wish to be immensely rich."

"Well, then, go along and find them. That is all you have to do; go and find them, and then you have them."

"But I don't know where to go."

"Well, if you will find a river that runs through white sands, between high mountains, in those white sands you will always find diamonds."

"I don't believe there is any such river."

"Oh yes, there are plenty of them. All you have to do is to go and find them, and then you have them."

Said Ali Hafed, "I will go."

So he sold his farm, collected his money, left his family in charge of a neighbor, and away he went in search of diamonds. He began his search, very properly to my mind, at the Mountains of the Moon. Afterward he came around into Palestine, then wandered on into Europe, and at last when his money was all spent and he was in rags, wretchedness and poverty, he stood on the shore of that bay at Barcelona, in Spain, when a great tidal wave came rolling in between the pillars of Hercules; and the poor, afflicted, suffering, dying man could not resist the awful temptation to cast himself into that incoming tide, and he sank beneath its foaming crest, never to rise in this life again.

When that old guide had told me that awfully sad story, he stopped the camel I was riding on and went back to fix the baggage that was coming off another camel, and I had an opportunity to muse over his story while he was gone. I remember saying to myself, "Why did he reserve that story for his 'particular friends'?" There seemed to be no beginning, no middle, no end, nothing to it. That was the first story I had ever heard told in my life, and would be the first one I ever read, in which the hero was killed in the first chapter. I had but one chapter of that story, and the hero was dead.

When the guide came back and took up the halter of my camel, he went right ahead with the story, into the second chapter, just as though there had been no break. The man who purchased Ali Hafed's farm one day led his camel into the garden to drink, and as that camel put its nose into the shallow water of that garden brook, Ali Hafed's successor noticed a curious flash of light from the white sands of the stream. He pulled out a black stone having an eye of light reflecting all the hues of the rainbow. He took the pebble into the house and put it on the mantel which covers the central fires, and forgot all about it.

A few days later this same old priest came in to visit Ali Hafed's successor, and the moment he opened that drawing room door, he saw that flash of light on the mantel, and he rushed up to it and shouted, "Here is a diamond! Has Ali Hafed returned?"

"Oh no, Ali Hafed has not returned, and that is not a diamond. That is nothing but a stone we found right out here in our own garden."

"But," said the priest, "I tell you I know a diamond when I see it. I know positively that is a diamond."

Then together they rushed out into that old garden and stirred up the white sands with their fingers, and lo! there came up other more beautiful and valuable gems than the first. "Thus," said the guide to me, and, friends, it is historically true, "was discovered the diamond mine of Golconda, the most magnificent diamond mine in all the history of mankind, excelling the Kimberley itself.

The Kohinoor, and the Orloff of the crown jewels of England and Russia, the largest on earth, came from that mine."

When that old Arab guide told me the second chapter of his story, he then took off his Turkish cap and swung it around in the air again to get my attention to the moral. Those Arab guides have morals to their stories, although they are not always moral. As he swung his hat, he said to me, "Had Ali Hafed remained at home and dug in his own cellar, or underneath his own wheat fields, or in his own garden, instead of wretchedness, starvation and death by suicide in a strange land, he would have had 'acres of diamonds.' For every acre of that old farm, yes, every shovelful, afterward revealed gems which since have decorated the crowns of monarchs."

When he had added the moral to his story, I saw why he re-served it for "his particular friends." But I did not tell him I could see it. It was that mean old Arab's way of going around a thing like a lawyer, to say indirectly what he did not dare say directly, that "in his private opinion there was a certain young man then traveling down the Tigris River that might better be at home in America." I did not tell him I could see that, but I told him his story reminded me of one, and I told it to him quick, and I think I will tell it to you.

I told him of a man out in California in 1847, who owned a ranch. He heard they had discovered gold in southern California, and so with a passion for gold he sold his ranch to Colonel Sutter, and away he went, never to come back. Colonel Sutter put a mill upon a stream that ran through that ranch, and one day his little girl brought some wet sand from the raceway into their home and sifted it through her fingers before the fire, and in that falling sand a visitor saw the first shining scales of real gold that were ever discovered in California. The man who had owned that ranch wanted gold, and he could have secured it for the mere taking. Indeed, 38 millions of dollars have been taken out of a very few acres since then. About eight years ago I delivered this lecture in a city that stands on that farm, and they told me that a one-third owner for years and years had been getting one hundred and twenty dollars in gold every fifteen minutes, sleeping or waking, without taxation. You and I would enjoy an income like that—if we didn't have to pay an income tax.

But a better illustration really than that occurred here in our own Pennsylvania. If there is anything I enjoy above another on the platform, it is to get one of these German audiences in Pennsylvania before me, and fire that at them, and I enjoy it to-night. There was a man living in Pennsylvania, not unlike some Pennsylvanians you have seen, who owned a farm, and he did with that farm just what I should do with a farm if I owned one in Pennsylvania—he sold it. But before he sold it he decided to secure employment collecting coal oil for his cousin, who was in the business in Canada, where they first discovered oil on this continent. They dipped it from the running streams at that early time. So this Pennsylvania farmer wrote to his cousin asking for employment. You see, friends, this farmer was not altogether a foolish man. No, he was not. He did not leave his farm until he had something else to do. *Of all the simpletons the stars shine on I don't know of a worse one than the man who leaves one job before he has gotten another.* That has especial reference to my profession, and has no reference whatever to a man seeking a divorce. When he wrote to his cousin for employment, his cousin replied, "I cannot engage you because you know nothing about the oil business."

Well, then the old farmer said, "I will know," and with most commendable zeal (characteristic of the students of Temple University) he set himself at the study of the whole subject. He began away back at the second day of God's creation when this world was covered thick and deep with that rich vegetation which since has turned to the primitive beds of coal. He studied the subject until he found that the drainings really of those rich beds of coal furnished the coal oil that was worth pumping, and then he found how it came up with the living springs. He studied until he knew what it looked like, smelled like, tasted like, and how to refine it. Now said he in his letter to his cousin, "I understand the oil business."

His cousin answered, "All right, come on."

So he sold his farm, according to the county record, for $833 (even money, "no cents"). He had scarcely gone from that place before the man who purchased the spot went out to arrange for the watering of the cattle. He found the previous owner had gone out years before and put a plank across the brook back of the barn, edgewise into the surface of the water just a few inches. The purpose of that plank at that sharp angle across the brook was to throw over to the other bank a dreadful-looking scum through which the cattle would not put their noses. But with that plank there to throw it all over to one side, the cattle would drink below, and thus that man who had gone to Canada had been himself damming back for 23 years a flood of coal oil which the state geologists of Pennsylvania declared to us ten years later was even then worth a hundred millions of dollars to our state, and four years ago our geologist declared the discovery to be worth to our state a thousand millions of dollars. The man who owned that territory on which the city of Titusville now stands, and those Pleasantville valleys, had studied the subject from the second day of God's creation clear down to the present time. He studied it until he knew all about it, and yet he is said to have sold the whole of it for $833 and, again I say, "no sense."

But I need another illustration. I found it in Massachusetts, and I am sorry I did because that is the state I came from. This young man in Massachusetts furnishes just another phase of my thought. He went to Yale College and studied mines and mining and became such an adept as a mining engineer that he was employed by the authorities of the university to train students who were behind in their classes. During his senior year he earned $15 a week for doing that work. When he graduated they raised his pay from $15 to $45 a week and offered him a professorship, and as soon as they did he went right home to his mother. *If they had raised that boy's pay from $15 to $15.60, he would have stayed and been proud of the place, but when they put it up to $45 at one leap, he said, "Mother, I won't work for $45 a week. The idea of a man with a brain like mine working for $45 a week!* Let's go out in California and stake out gold mines and silver mines and be immensely rich."

Said his mother, "Now, Charlie, it is just as well to be happy as it is to be rich."

"Yes," said Charlie, "but it is just as well to be rich and happy, too." And they were both right about it. As he was an only son and she a widow, of course he had his way. They always do.

They sold out in Massachusetts, and instead of going to California they went to Wisconsin, where he went into the employ of the Superior Copper Mining Company at $15 a week again, but with the proviso in his contract that he should have an interest in any mines he should discover for the company. I don't believe he ever discovered a mine, and if I am looking in the face of any stockholder of that copper company, you wish he had discovered something or other. I have friends who are not here because they could not afford a ticket, who did have stock in that company at the time this young man was employed there. This young man went out there, and I have not heard a word from him. I don't know what became of him, and I don't know whether he found any mines or not, but I don't believe he ever did.

But I do know the other end of the line. He had scarcely gotten out of the old homestead before the succeeding owner went out to dig potatoes. The potatoes were already growing in the ground when he bought the farm, and as the old farmer was bringing in a basket of potatoes, it hugged very tight between the ends of the stone fence. You know in Massachusetts our farms are nearly all stone wall. There you are obliged to be very economical of front gateways in order to have some place to put the stone. When that basket hugged so tight, he set it down on the ground, and then dragged on one side, and pulled on the other side, and as he was dragging that basket through, this farmer noticed in the upper and outer corner of that stone wall, right next the gate, a block of native silver eight inches square. That professor of mines, mining and mineralogy who knew so much about the subject that he would not work for $45 a week, when he sold that homestead in Massachusetts, sat right on that silver to make the bargain. He was born on that homestead, was brought up there and had gone back and forth rubbing the stone with his sleeve until it reflected his countenance, and seemed to say, "Here is a hundred thousand dollars right down here just for the taking." But he would not take it. It was in a home in Newburyport, Massachusetts, and there was no silver there, all away off—well, I don't know where, and he did not, but somewhere else, and he was a professor of mineralogy.

My friends, that mistake is very universally made, and why should we even smile at him. I often wonder what has become of him. I do not know at all, but I will tell you what I "guess" as a Yankee. I guess that he sits out there by his fireside tonight with his friends gathered around him, and he is saying to them something like this: "Do you know that man Conwell who lives in Philadelphia?"

"Oh yes, I have heard of him."

"Do you know that man Jones that lives in Philadelphia?"

"Yes, I have heard of him, too."

Then he begins to laugh, and shakes his sides, and says to his friends, "Well, they have done just the same thing I did, precisely"—and that spoils the whole joke, for you and I have done the same thing he did, and while we sit here and laugh at him, he has a better right to sit out there and laugh at us. I know I have made the same mistakes, but, of course, that does not make any difference, because we don't expect the same man to preach and practice, too.

As I come here tonight and look around this audience, I am seeing again what through these fifty years I have continually seen—men that are making precisely that same mistake. I often wish I could see the younger people, and would that the Academy had been filled tonight with our high school scholars and our grammar school scholars, that I could have them to talk to. While I would have preferred such an audience as that—because they are most susceptible, as they have not grown up into their prejudices as we have, they have not gotten into any custom that they cannot break, they have not met with any failures as we have—and while I could perhaps do such an audience as that more good than I can do grown-up people, yet I will do the best I can with the material I have. I say to you that you have "acres of diamonds" in Philadelphia right where you now live.

"Oh," but you will say, "you cannot know much about your city if you think there are any 'acres of diamonds' here."

I was greatly interested in that account in the newspaper of the young man who found that diamond in North Carolina. It was one of the purest diamonds that has ever been discovered, and it has several predecessors near the same locality. I went to a distinguished professor in mineralogy and asked him where he thought those diamonds came from. The professor secured the map of the geologic formations of our continent and traced it. He said it went either through the underlying carboniferous strata adapted for such production, westward through Ohio and the Mississippi, or in more probability came eastward through Virginia and up the shore of the Atlantic Ocean. It is a fact that the diamonds were there, for they have been discovered and sold; and that they were carried down there during the drift period, from some northern locality. Now who can say but some person going down with his drill in Philadelphia will find some trace of a diamond mine yet down here? Oh, friends! you cannot say that you are not over one of the greatest diamond mines in the world, for such a diamond as that only comes from the most profitable mines that are found on earth.

But it serves simply to illustrate my thought, which I emphasize by saying if you do not have the actual diamond mines literally, you have all that they would be good for to you. Because now that the Queen of England has given the greatest compliment ever conferred upon an American woman for her attire because she did not appear with any jewels at all at the late reception in England, it has almost done away with the use of diamonds anyhow. All you would care for would be the few you would wear if you wish to be modest, and the rest you would sell for money. . . .

But let me hasten to one other greater thought. "Show me the great men and women who live in Philadelphia." A gentleman over there will get up and say, "We don't have any great men in Philadelphia. They don't live here. They live away off in Rome or St. Petersburg or London or Manayunk, or anywhere else but here in our town." I have come now to the apex of my thought. I have come now to the heart of the whole matter and to the center of my struggle: Why isn't Philadelphia a greater city in its greater wealth? Why does New York excel Philadelphia? People say, "Because of her harbor." Why do many other cities of the United States get ahead of Philadelphia now? There is only one answer, and that is because our own people talk down their own city. If there ever was a community on earth that has to be forced ahead, it is the city of Philadelphia. If we are to have a boulevard, talk it down; if we are going to have better schools, talk them down; if you wish to have wise legislation, talk it down; talk all the proposed improvements down. That is the only great wrong that I can lay at the feet of the magnificent Philadelphia that has been so universally kind to me. I say it is time we turn around in our city and begin to talk up the things that are in our city, and begin to set them before the world as the people of Chicago, New York, St. Louis and San Francisco do. Oh, if we only could get that spirit out among our people, that we can do things in Philadelphia and do them well!

Arise, ye millions of Philadelphians, trust in God and man, and believe in the great opportunities that are right here—not over in New York or Boston, but here—for business, for everything that is worth living for on earth. There was never an opportunity greater. Let us talk up our own city. . . .

Oh, I learned the lesson then that I will never forget so long as the tongue of the bell of time continues to swing for me. Greatness consists not in the holding of some future office, but really consists in doing great deeds with little means and the accomplishment of vast purposes from the private ranks of life. To be great at all one must be great here, now, in Philadelphia. He who can give to this city better streets and better sidewalks, better schools and more colleges, more happiness and more civilization, more of God, he will be great anywhere. Let every man or woman here, if you never hear me again, remember this, that if you wish to be great at all, you must begin where you are and what you are, in Philadelphia, now. He that can give to his city any blessing, he who can be a good citizen while he lives here, he that can make better homes, he that can be a blessing whether he works in the shop or sits behind the counter or keeps house, whatever be his life, he who would be great anywhere must first be great in his own Philadelphia.

Notes

Introduction

1. A. Cheree Carlson, "Narrative as the Philosopher's Stone: How Russell H. Conwell Changed Lead into Diamonds," *Western Journal of Speech Communication* 53 (Fall 1989): 342–355.

2. I have included the text of Conwell's speech in the appendix.

3. See Genesis 13:8–9.

4. Genesis 13:16–17.

5. See Genesis 15:5.

6. See Luke 23:42–43.

Chapter 1 Why Not Now?

1. Randy Alfred, "Nov. 18, 1993: Railroad Time Goes Coast to Coast," *Wired*, November 18, 2010, https://www.wired.com/2010/11/1118railroad-time-zones/.

2. Fran Capo, *It Happened in New Jersey* (Guilford, Conn.: Globe Pequot Press, 2004), 69.

3. "Paxson Opts Out of TV Deal," *Variety*, April 3, 1997, https://variety.com/1997/scene/vpage/paxson-opts-out-of-tv-deal-1117435009/.

4. See John 2:4–5.

5. See Hebrews 13:8.

6. See John 11:21–26.

7. Deuteronomy 33:25.

8. See Ecclesiastes 9:4.

Chapter 2 How Diamonds Are Born

1. See Exodus 33:11.

2. This story has been told in numerous variations for more than a hundred years, perhaps most notably by Abigail Van Buren (Dear Abby) in her column. Abigail Van Buren, "Modern Parable Teaches Lesson about Gratitude," Dear Abby (syndicated column), July 12, 1996, https://www.uexpress.com/dearabby/1996/7/12/modern-parable-teaches-lesson-about-gratitude.

3. Job 23:8–9.

4. Job 19:25.

5. Genesis 50:19–20.

6. Romans 8:28.

7. See Joshua 1:8.

Chapter 3 The "Stay Here" Command

1. "The History of Tabasco Brand," McIlhenny Company, accessed June 25, 2019, https://www.tabasco.com/tabasco-history/.

2. "What You Never Knew about Tabasco Sauce" (video), *Smithsonian Magazine*, accessed June 25, 2019, https://www.smithsonianmag.com/videos/category/arts-culture/what-you-never-knew-about-tabasco-sauce/.

3. See Genesis 12:10.

4. See Numbers 21:4–5.

5. Numbers 21:17–18 esv.

6. Nick Paumgarten, "The $40-Million Elbow," *The New Yorker*, October 15, 2006, https://www.newyorker.com/magazine/2006/10/23/the-40-million-elbow.

7. Hallie Detrick, "A Picasso Painting Owned by Steve Wynn Was Damaged—Again," *Fortune*, May 14, 2018, http://fortune.com/2018/05/14/steve-wynn-picasso-painting/.

8. Eyder Peralta, "Years after the Elbow Incident, Steve Wynn Sells Picasso's 'Le Rêve' for $155 Million," *The Two-Way* (blog), March 26, 2013, https://www.npr.org/sections/the-two-way/2013/03/26/175412881/years-after-the-elbow-incident-steve-wynn-sells-picassos-le-r-ve-for-155-million.

9. See Joel 2:25.

10. Amy Ellis Nutt, "Suicide Rates Rise Sharply across the United States, New Report Shows," *Washington Post*, June 7, 2018, https://www.washingtonpost.com/news/to-your-health/wp/2018/06/07/u-s-suicide-rates-rise-sharply-across-the-country-new-report-shows/?utm_term=.68d0f2dbe9fa.

Chapter 4 Open My Eyes

1. See 2 Kings 6:14–16.

2. Marina Chapman, *The Girl with No Name: The Incredible Story of a Child Raised by Monkeys* (New York: Pegasus Books, 2013), Kindle edition, chapter 8.

3. See Deuteronomy 28:13.

4. See Isaiah 62:3.

5. See Psalm 139:14.

6. See 2 Corinthians 5:17.

7. See Genesis 15:5.

8. See Judges 7:9–11.

9. See Judges 7:13–14.

10. Jim Flick and Jack Nicklaus, "Jim Flick and Jack Nicklaus: Go to the Movies," *Golf Digest*, April 27, 2010, https://www.golfdigest.com/story/flick-nicklaus-film.

11. George Sylvester Viereck, "What Life Means to Einstein," *Saturday Evening Post*, October 26, 1929, http://www.saturdayeveningpost.com/wp-content/uploads/satevepost/what_life_means_to_einstein.pdf.

Chapter 5 Hell in the Hallway

1. Psalm 24:7–8.

2. See John 10:10.

3. See Joshua 5:15.

4. "Jabez," *Bible Study Tools*, accessed June 11, 2019, https://www.behindthename.com /name/jabez

5. 1 Chronicles 4:10.

6. See 2 Chronicles 20:21.

7. Gerald Horton Bath, "Long Walk." In *My Christmas Treasury*, ed. by Norman Vincent Peale, 146–147. San Francisco: HarperSanFrancisco, 1991.

Chapter 6 Let It Take You Up

1. Matthew 3:10.

2. Galatians 5:22–23.

3. Psalm 92:12–15.

Chapter 7 Let Down Your Bucket

1. Booker T. Washington, "Cast Down Your Bucket Where You Are" (speech presented at the Cotton States and International Exposition, Atlanta, GA, September 18, 1895), http:// historymatters.gmu.edu/d/88/.

2. "Report 'Anchoring Mistake' to Blame for Fatal Boating Accident," *Peoria Journal Star*, March 28, 2009, https://www.pjstar.com/article/20090328/NEWS/303289890.

3. Max Lucado, *Six Hours One Friday* (Nashville: W Publishing Group, 2004), 2.

4. See Acts 27:29.

5. Acts 27:24.

6. Psalm 133:1–2.

7. See Psalm 84:11.

Chapter 8 Focus on the Positive

1. See Numbers 13:20.

2. See Numbers 14:37.

3. See Numbers 13:28.

4. See Numbers 14:1.

5. See Numbers 14:37.

6. See Numbers 14:20–23.

7. See Numbers 14:24.

8. 1 Corinthians 2:9.

9. Hebrews 6:10.

Chapter 9 Take This Job and Love It

1. See Genesis 2:15.

2. Daniel 6:3.

3. See Zechariah 4:10.

Chapter 10 How to Be a Hero

1. See Joshua 2:12–13.

2. Proverbs 28:20.

3. World Triathlon Corporation, "Video: A Tribute to Team Hoyt," June 5, 2018, http://www.ironman.com/media-library/videos/2018/40th-videos/team-hoyt.aspx#axzz5u2qsoLbJ.

Chapter 11 If You're in It, You Can Win It

1. See Exodus 13:17–18.
2. Ezekiel 37:1.
3. Joshua 24:15.
4. "Then the LORD said to me, 'You have seen well, for I am [actively] watching over My word to fulfill it'" (Jeremiah 1:12 AMP).
5. See Daniel 9:1–4.

Chapter 12 Heaven, the Ultimate Acres of Diamonds

1. C. S. Lewis, *Mere Christianity* (New York: HarperOne, 2015), 134.
2. See Revelation 4:1.
3. See Revelation 5:11.
4. See Ephesians 3:15.
5. See 1 John 3:2.
6. See Revelation 21:1.

Appendix

1. The text of this speech comes from Russell H. Conwell, *Acres of Diamonds* (New York: Harper & Brothers, 1915), vol. 2, http://www.gutenberg.org/files/34258/34258-h/34258-h.htm.

Jentezen Franklin Jentezen Franklin is the senior pastor of Free Chapel, a multicampus church based in Gainesville, Georgia, with seven campuses in three states. Each week his television program, *Kingdom Connection*, is broadcast on major networks to millions of homes all over the world. In addition to speaking at conferences worldwide, he is also a *New York Times* bestselling author, having written numerous books, including his most recent bestseller, *Love Like You've Never Been Hurt*.

Jentezen and his wife, Cherise, have been married 32 years, have five children and four grandchildren, and make their home in Gainesville, Georgia.

More Powerful Teaching from Jentezen Franklin!

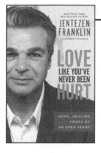